P9-CCV-599

Modern Critical Interpretations

Homer's
The Iliad

Modern Critical Interpretations

These and other titles in preparation

Modern Critical Interpretations

Homer's
The Iliad

Edited and with an introduction by
Harold Bloom
Sterling Professor of the Humanities
Yale University

Chelsea House Publishers
NEW YORK ◊ PHILADELPHIA

© 1987 by Chelsea House Publishers,
a division of Main Line Book Co.

Introduction © 1987 by Harold Bloom

All rights reserved. No part of this publication may be
reproduced or transmitted in any form or by any means
without the written permission of the publisher.

Printed and bound in the United States of America

10 9 8 7 6 5 4

∞ The paper used in this publication meets the minimum
requirements of the American National Standard for Permanence
of Paper for Printed Library Materials, Z39.48-1984.

Library of Congress Cataloging-in-Publication Data

Homer's Iliad.

(Modern critical interpretations)
Bibliography: p.
Includes index.
1. Homer. Iliad.   I. Bloom, Harold.   II. Series.
PA4037.A5H8   1987   883′.01   86–33440
ISBN 0–87754–912–5

Contents

Editor's Note

This book gathers together a representative selection of the best modern criticism of Homer's *Iliad,* arranged in the chronological order of its original publication. I am grateful to Marena Fisher for her erudition and judgment as a researcher.

My introduction compares and contrasts the poet of the *Iliad* and the Yahwist or J writer, author of the oldest narrative strand in Genesis, Exodus, Numbers. The chronological sequence begins with E. R. Dodds and Bruno Snell, who taught modern readers how to accommodate themselves to irrational (Dodds) and nonrational (Snell) elements in Homer's view of man. Placed between them is Cedric Whitman's masterly puzzling-out of the possible relation between the Homeric representation of character and the largely unknown pre-Homeric tradition.

Eric Havelock's incisive view of the Homeric state of mind is complemented by James M. Redfield's account of Homeric culture as the purification of nature and the *Iliad* as the purification of culture. A second essay by Havelock examines the function of fantasy in the Homeric depiction of the hero, a theme that is explored further in Gregory Nagy's consideration of Achilles as the best of the Achaeans.

In this book's final essay, Jeffrey Hurwit relates Homer's view of man, partly as expounded by Snell, to the Dipylon style of vase painting, and so achieves a fresh insight into the ordered sensibility of mid-eighth-century Greece.

Introduction

Hektor in his ecstasy of power
is mad for battle, confident in Zeus,
deferring to neither men nor gods. Pure frenzy
fills him, and he prays for the bright dawn
when he will shear our stern-post beaks away
and fire all our ships, while in the shipways
amid that holocaust he carries death
among our men, driven out by smoke. All this
I gravely fear; I fear the gods will make
good his threatenings, and our fate will be
to die here, far from the pastureland of Argos.
Rouse yourself, if even at this hour
you'll pitch in for the Akhaians and deliver them
from Trojan havoc. In the years to come
this day will be remembered pain for you
if you do not.
                    Iliad, Fitzgerald translation, bk. 9, ll. 237–50

For the divisions of Reuben there were great thoughts of heart.
   Why abidest thou among the sheepfolds, to hear the bleatings of the flocks?
For the divisions of Reuben there were great searchings of heart.
   Gilead abode beyond Jordan: and why did Dan remain in ships? Asher
continued on the sea shore, and abode in his breaches.
   Zebulun and Naphtali were a people that jeoparded their lives unto the
death in the high places of the field.
                                                   Judges 5:15–18

I

Simone Weil loved both the *Iliad* and the Gospels, and rather oddly associated them, as though Jesus had been a Greek and not a Jew:

The Gospels are the last marvelous expression of the Greek genius, as the *Iliad* is the first . . . with the Hebrews, misfortune

1

was a sure indication of sin and hence a legitimate object of contempt; to them a vanquished enemy was abhorrent to God himself and condemned to expiate all sorts of crimes—this is a view that makes cruelty permissible and indeed indispensable. And no text of the Old Testament strikes a note comparable to the note heard in the Greek epic, unless it be certain parts of the book of Job. Throughout twenty centuries of Christianity, the Romans and the Hebrews have been admired, read, imitated, both in deed and word; their masterpieces have yielded an appropriate quotation every time anybody had a crime he wanted to justify.

Though vicious in regard to the Hebrew Bible, this is also merely banal, being another in that weary procession of instances of Jewish self-hatred, and even of Christian anti-Semitism. What is interesting in it however is Weil's strong misreading of the *Iliad* as "the poem of force," as when she said: "Its bitterness is the only justifiable bitterness, for it springs from the subjections of the human spirit to force, that is, in the last analysis, to matter." Of what "human spirit" did Weil speak? That sense of the spirit is of course Hebraic, and not at all Greek, and is totally alien to the text of the *Iliad*. Cast in Homer's terms, her sentence should have ascribed justifiable bitterness, the bitterness of Achilles and Hector, to "the subjections of the human force to the gods' force and to fate's force." For that is how Homer sees men; they are not spirits imprisoned in matter but forces or drives that live, perceive, and feel. I adopt here Bruno Snell's famous account of "Homer's view of man," in which Achilles, Hector and all the other heroes, even Odysseus, "consider themselves a battleground of arbitrary forces and uncanny powers." Abraham, Jacob, Joseph and Moses clearly do not view themselves as a site where arbitrary forces clash in battle, and neither of course does David or his possible descendant, Jesus. The *Iliad* is as certainly the poem of force as Genesis, Exodus, Numbers is the poem of the will of Yahweh, who has his arbitrary and uncanny aspects but whose force is justice and whose power is also canny.

II

The poet of the *Iliad* seems to me to have only one ancient rival, the prime and original author of much of Genesis, Exodus, Numbers, known as the Yahwist or J writer to scholars. Homer and J have absolutely nothing in common except their uncanny sublimity, and they are sublime in very different modes. In a profound sense, they are agonists, though neither ever heard of the other, or listened to the other's texts. They compete for the consciousness of Western nations, and their belated strife may be the largest single factor that makes for a divided sensibility in the literature and life of the West. For what marks the West is its troubled sense that its cognition goes one way, and its spiritual life goes in quite another. We have no ways of thinking that are not Greek, and yet our morality and religion—outer and inner—find their ultimate source in the Hebrew Bible.

The burden of the word of the Lord, as delivered by Zechariah (9:12–13) has been prophetic of the cultural civil war that, for us, can never end:

> Turn you to the stronghold, ye prisoners of hope: even today do
> I declare that I will render double unto thee;
>   When I have bent Judah for me, filled the bow of Ephraim,
> and raised up thy sons, O Zion, against thy sons, O Greece, and
> made thee as the sword of a mighty man.

Like the Hebrew Bible, Homer is both scripture and book of general knowledge, and these are necessarily still the prime educational texts, with only Shakespeare making a third, a third who evidences most deeply the split between Greek cognition and Hebraic spirituality. To read the *Iliad* in particular without distorting it is now perhaps impossible, and for reasons that transcend the differences between Homer's language and implicit socio-economic structure, and our own. The true difference, whether we are Gentile or Jew, believer or skeptic, Hegelian or Freudian, is between Yahweh, and the tangled company of Zeus and the Olympians, fate and the daemonic world. Christian, Moslem, Jew or their mixed descendants, we are children of Abraham and not of Achilles. Homer is perhaps most powerful when he represents the strife of men and gods. The Yahwist or J is as powerful when he shows us Jacob wrestling a nameless one among the Elohim to a standstill, but the instance is unique, and Jacob struggles, not to overcome the nameless one, but to delay him. And Jacob is no Heracles; he wrestles out of character, as it were, so as to give us a giant trope for Israel's persistence in its endless quest for a time without boundaries.

The *Iliad,* except for the Yahwist, Dante, and Shakespeare, is the most extraordinary writing yet to come out of the West, but how much of it is spiritually acceptable to us, or would be, if we pondered it closely? Achilles and Hector are hardly the same figure, since we cannot visualize Achilles living a day-to-day life in a city, but they are equally glorifiers of battle. Defensive warfare is no more an ideal (for most of us) than is aggression, but in the *Iliad* both are very near to the highest good, which is victory.

What other ultimate value is imaginable in a world where the ordinary reality is battle? It is true that the narrator, and his personages, are haunted by similes of peace, but, as James M. Redfield observes, the rhetorical purpose of these similes "is not to describe the world of peace but to make vivid the world of war." Indeed, the world of peace, in the *Iliad,* is essentially a war between humans and nature, in which farmers rip out the grain and fruit as so many spoils of battle. This helps explain why the *Iliad* need not bother to praise war, since reality is a constant contest anyway, in which nothing of value can be attained without despoiling or ruining someone or something else.

To compete for the foremost place was the Homeric ideal, which is not exactly the biblical ideal of honoring your father and your mother. I find it difficult to read the *Iliad* as "the tragedy of Hector," as Redfield and others do. Hector is stripped of tragic dignity, indeed very nearly of all dignity, before he dies. The epic is the tragedy of Achilles, ironically enough, because he retains the foremost place, yet cannot overcome the bitterness of his sense of his own mortality. To be only half a god appears to be Homer's implicit definition of what makes a hero tragic. But this is not tragedy in the biblical sense, where the dilemma of Abraham arguing with Yahweh on the road to Sodom, or of Jacob wrestling with the angel of death, is the need to act as if one were everything in oneself while knowing also that, compared to Yahweh, one is nothing in oneself. Achilles can neither act as if he were everything in himself, nor can he believe that, compared even to Zeus, he is nothing in himself. Abraham and Jacob therefore, and not Achilles, are the cultural ancestors of Hamlet and the other Shakespearean heroes.

What after all is it to be the "best of the Achaeans," Achilles, as contrasted to the comparable figure, David (who in Yahweh's eyes is clearly the best among the children of Abraham)? It is certainly not to be the most complete man among them. That, as James Joyce rightly concluded, is certainly Odysseus. The best of the Achaeans is the one who can kill Hector, which is to say that Achilles, in an American heroic context, would have been the fastest gun in the West. Perhaps David would have been that also, and certainly David mourns Jonathan as Achilles mourns Patroklos, which reminds us that David and Achilles both are poets. But Achilles, sulking in his tent, is palpably a child, with a wavering vision of himself, inevitable since his vitality, his perception, and his affective life are all divided from one another, as Bruno Snell demonstrated. David, even as a child, is a mature and autonomous ego, with his sense of life, his vision of other selves, and his emotional nature all integrated into a new kind of man, the hero whom Yahweh had decided not only to love, but to make immortal *through his descendants,* who would never lose Yahweh's favor. Jesus, *contra* Simone Weil, can only be the descendant of David, and not of Achilles. Or to put it most simply, Achilles is the son of a goddess, but David is a Son of God.

III

The single "modern" author who compels comparison with the poet of the *Iliad* and the writer of the J text is Tolstoy, whether in *War and Peace* or in the short novel which is the masterpiece of his old age, *Hadji Murad*. Rachel Bespaloff, in her essay *On the Iliad* (rightly commended by the superb Homeric translator, Robert Fitzgerald, as conveying how distant, how re-fined the art of Homer was) seems to have fallen into the error of believing that the Bible and Homer, since both resemble Tolstoy, must also resemble one another. Homer and Tolstoy share the extraordinary balance between the individual in action and groups in action that alone permits the epic accurately to represent battle. The Yahwist and Tolstoy share an uncanny mode of irony that turns upon the incongruities of incommensurable entities, Yahweh or universal history, and man, meeting in violent confrontation or juxtaposition. But the Yahwist has little interest in groups; he turns away in some disdain when the blessing, on Sinai, is transferred from an elite to the mass of the people. And the clash of gods and men, or of fate and the hero, remains in Homer a conflict between forces not wholly incommensurable, though the hero must die, whether in or beyond the poem.

The crucial difference between the Yahwist and Homer, aside from their representations of the self, necessarily is the indescribable difference between Yahweh and Zeus. Both are personalities, but such an assertion becomes an absurdity directly they are juxtaposed. Erich Auerbach, com-paring the poet of the *Odyssey* and the Elohist, the Yahwist's revisionist, traced the mimetic difference between the *Odyssey*'s emphasis upon "fore-grounding" and the Bible's reliance upon the authority of an implied "back-grounding." There is something to that distinction, but it tends to fade out when we move from the *Odyssey* to the *Iliad* and from the Elohist to the Yahwist. The *Iliad* may not demand interpretation as much as the Yahwist does, but it hardly can be apprehended without any reader's considerable labor of aesthetic contextualization. Its man, unlike the Yahwist's, has little in common with the "psychological man" of Freud.

Joseph, who may have been the Yahwist's portrait of King David, provides a fascinating post-Oedipal contrast to his father Jacob, but Achilles seems never to have approached any relation whatever to his father Peleus, who is simply a type of ignoble old age wasting towards the wrong kind of death. Surely the most striking contrast between the *Iliad* and the J text is that between the mourning of Priam and the grief of Jacob when he believes Joseph to be dead. Old men in Homer are good mostly for grieving, but in the Yahwist they represent the wisdom and the virtue of the fathers. Yahweh is the God of Abraham, the God of Isaac, the God of Jacob, even as He will be the God of Moses, the God of David, the God of Jesus. But Zeus is nobody's god, as it were, and Achilles might as well not have had a father at all.

Priam's dignity is partly redeemed when his mourning for Hector is joined to that of Achilles for Patroklos, but the aged Jacob is dignity itself, as his grandfather Abraham was before him. Nietzsche's characterization is just. A people whose ideal is the agon for the foremost place must fall behind in honoring their parents, while a people who exalt fatherhood and motherhood will transfer the agon to the temporal realm, to struggle there not for being the best at one time, but rather for inheriting the blessing, which promises more life in a time without boundaries.

Yahweh is the source of the blessing, and Yahweh, though frequently enigmatic in J, is never an indifferent onlooker. No Hebrew writer could conceive of a Yahweh who is essentially an audience, whether indifferent or engrossed. Homer's gods are human—all-too-human—particularly in their abominable capacity to observe suffering almost as a kind of sport. The Yahweh of Amos and the prophets after him could not be further from Homer's Olympian Zeus.

It can be argued that the spectatorship of the gods gives Homer an immense aesthetic advantage over the writers of the Hebrew Bible. The sense of a divine audience constantly in attendance both provides a fascinating interplay with Homer's human auditors, and guarantees that Achilles and Hector will perform in front of a sublimity greater even than their own. To have the gods as one's audience enhances and honors the heroes who are Homer's prime actors. Yahweh frequently hides Himself, and will not be there when you cry out for Him, or He may call out your name unexpectedly, to which you can only respond: "Here I am." Zeus is capricious and is finally limited by fate. Yahweh surprises you, and has no limitation. He will not lend you dignity by serving as your audience, and yet He is anything but indifferent to you. He fashioned you out of the moistened red clay, and then blew his own breath into your nostrils, so as to make you a living being. You grieve Him or you please Him, but fundamentally He is your longing for the father, as Freud insisted. Zeus is not your longing for anyone, and he will not save you even if you are Heracles, his own son.

IV

In Homer, you fight to be the best, to take away the women of the enemy, and to survive as long as possible, short of aging into ignoble decrepitude. That is not why you fight in the Hebrew Bible. There you fight the wars of Yahweh, which so appalled that harsh saint, Simone Weil. I want to close this introduction by comparing two great battle odes, the war song of Deborah and Barak, in Judges 5, and the astonishing passage in book 18 of the *Iliad* when Achilles reenters the scene of battle, in order to recover his arms, his armor, and the body of Patroklos:

> At this,
> Iris left him, running downwind. Akhilleus,
> whom Zeus loved, now rose. Around his shoulders
> Athena hung her shield, like a thunderhead
> with trailing fringe. Goddess of goddesses,
> she bound his head with golden cloud, and made
> his very body blaze with fiery light.
> Imagine how the pyre of a burning town
> will tower to heaven and be seen for miles
> from the island under attack, while all day long
> outside their town, in brutal combat, pikemen
> suffer the wargod's winnowing; at sundown
> flare on flare is lit, the signal fires
> shoot up for other islanders to see,
> that some relieving force in ships may come:
> just so the baleful radiance from Akhilleus
> lit the sky. Moving from parapet
> to moat, without a nod for the Akhaians,
> keeping clear, in deference to his mother,
> he halted and gave tongue. Not far from him
> Athena shrieked. The great sound shocked the Trojans
> into tumult, as a trumpet blown
> by a savage foe shocks an encircled town,
> so harsh and clarion was Akhilleus' cry.
> The hearts of men quailed, hearing that brazen voice.
> Teams, foreknowing danger, turned their cars
> and charioteers blanched, seeing unearthly fire,
> kindled by the grey-eyed goddess Athena,
> brilliant over Akhilleus. Three great cries
> he gave above the moat. Three times they shuddered,

> whirling backward, Trojans and allies,
> and twelve good men took mortal hurt
> from cars and weapons in the rank behind.
> Now the Akhaians leapt at the chance
> to bear Patroklos' body out of range.
> They placed it on his bed,
> and old companions there with brimming eyes
> surrounded him. Into their midst Akhilleus
> came then, and he wept hot tears to see
> his faithful friend, torn by the sharp spearhead,
> lying cold upon his cot. Alas,
> the man he sent to war with team and chariot
> he could not welcome back alive.

Exalted and burning with Athena's divine fire, the unarmed Achilles is more terrible even than the armed hero would be. It is his angry shouts that panic the Trojans, yet the answering shout of the goddess adds to their panic, since they realize that they face preternatural powers. When Yahweh roars, in the prophets Isaiah and Joel, the effect is very different, though He too cries out "like a man of war." The difference is in Homer's magnificent antiphony between man and goddess, Achilles and Athena. Isaiah would not have had the king and Yahweh exchanging battle shouts in mutual support, because of the shocking incommensurateness which does not apply to Achilles and Athena.

I began this introduction by juxtaposing two epigraphs, Odysseus shrewdly warning Achilles that "this day," on which Hector may burn the Achaean ships, "will be remembered pain for you," if Achilles does not return to the battle, and a superb passage from Deborah's war song in Judges 5. Hector's "ecstasy of power" would produce "remembered pain" for Achilles, as power must come at the expense of someone else's pain, and ecstasy results from the victory of inflicting *memorable* suffering. Memory depends upon pain, which was Nietzsche's fiercely Homeric analysis of all significant memory. But that is not the memory exalted in the Hebrew Bible. Deborah, with a bitter irony, laughs triumphantly at the tribes of Israel that did not assemble for the battle against Sisera, and most of all at Reuben, with its scruples, doubts, hesitations: "great searchings of heart." She scorns those who kept to business as usual, Dan who remained in ships, and Asher who continued on the sea shore. Then suddenly, with piercing intensity and moral force, she utters a great paean of praise and triumph, for the tribes that risked everything on behalf of their covenant with Yahweh, for those who transcended "great thoughts" and "great searchings of heart":

Zebulun and Naphtali were a people that jeoparded their lives
unto the death in the high places of the field.

The high places are both descriptive and honorific; they are where the
terms of the covenant were kept. Zebulun and Naphtali fight, not to be the
foremost among the tribes of Israel, and not to possess Sisera's women, but
to fulfill the terms of the covenant, to demonstrate *emunah,* which is trust in
Yahweh. Everyone in Homer knows better than to trust in Zeus. The
aesthetic supremacy of the *Iliad* again must be granted. Homer is the best of
the poets, and always will keep the foremost place. What he lacks, even
aesthetically, is a quality of trust in the transcendent memory of a covenant
fulfilled, a lack of the sublime hope that moves the Hebrew poet Deborah:

They fought from heaven; the stars in their courses fought against
Sisera.
The river of Kishon swept them away, that ancient river, the
river Kishon. O my soul, thou hast trodden down strength.

Agamemnon's Apology

E. R. Dodds

The recesses of feeling, the darker, blinder strata of character, are the only places in the world in which we catch real fact in the making.

WILLIAM JAMES

I shall begin by considering a particular aspect of Homeric religion. To some classical scholars the Homeric poems will seem a bad place to look for any sort of religious experience. "The truth is," says Professor Mazon in a recent book, "that there was never a poem less religious than the *Iliad*." This may be thought a little sweeping; but it reflects an opinion which seems to be widely accepted. Professor Murray thinks that the so-called Homeric religion "was not really religion at all"; for in his view "the real worship of Greece before the fourth century almost never attached itself to those luminous Olympian forms." Similarly Dr. Bowra observes that "this complete anthropomorphic system has *of course* no relation to real religion or to morality. These gods are a delightful, gay invention of poets."

Of course—if the expression "real religion" means the kind of thing that enlightened Europeans or Americans of today recognize as being religion. But if we restrict the meaning of the word in this way, are we not in danger of undervaluing, or even of overlooking altogether, certain types of experience which we no longer interpret in a religious sense, but which may nevertheless in their time have been quite heavily charged with religious significance? My purpose in the present chapter is not to quarrel with the distinguished scholars I have quoted over their use of terms, but to call attention to one kind of experience in Homer which is prima facie religious and to examine its psychology.

From *The Greeks and the Irrational.* © 1951 by the Regents of the University of California. University of California Press, 1951.

Let us start from that experience of divine temptation or infatuation (*atē*) which led Agamemnon to compensate himself for the loss of his own mistress by robbing Achilles of his. "Not I," he declared afterwards, "not I was the cause of this act, but Zeus and my portion and the Erinys who walks in darkness: they it was who in the assembly put wild *atē* in my understanding, on that day when I arbitrarily took Achilles' prize from him. So what could I do? Deity will always have its way." By impatient modern readers these words of Agamemnon's have sometimes been dismissed as a weak excuse or evasion of responsibility. But not, I think, by those who read carefully. An evasion of responsibility in the juridical sense the words certainly are not; for at the end of his speech Agamemnon offers compensation precisely on this ground—"But since I was blinded by *atē* and Zeus took away my understanding, I am willing to make my peace and give abundant compensation." Had he acted of his own volition, he could not so easily admit himself in the wrong; as it is, he will pay for his acts. Juridically, his position would be the same in either case; for early Greek justice cared nothing for intent—it was the act that mattered. Nor is he dishonestly inventing a moral alibi; for the victim of his action takes the same view of it as he does. "Father Zeus, great indeed are the *atai* thou givest to men. Else the son of Atreus would never have persisted in rousing the *thūmos* in my chest, nor obstinately taken the girl against my will." You may think that Achilles is here politely accepting a fiction, in order to save the High King's face? But no: for already in book 1, when Achilles is explaining the situation to Thetis, he speaks of Agamemnon's behaviour as his *atē*; and in book 9 he exclaims, "Let the son of Atreus go to his doom and not disturb me, for Zeus the counsellor took away his understanding." It is Achilles' view of the matter as much as Agamemnon's; and in the famous words which introduce the story of the Wrath—"The plan of Zeus was fulfilled"—we have a strong hint that it is also the poet's view.

If this were the only incident which Homer's characters interpreted in this peculiar way, we might hesitate as to the poet's motive: we might guess, for example, that he wished to avoid alienating the hearers' sympathy too completely from Agamemnon, or again that he was trying to impart a deeper significance to the rather undignified quarrel of the two chiefs by representing it as a step in the fulfillment of a divine plan. But these explanations do not apply to other passages where "the gods" or "some god" or Zeus are said to have momentarily "taken away" or "destroyed" or "ensorcelled" a human being's understanding. Either of them might indeed be applied to the case of Helen, who ends a deeply moving

and evidently sincere speech by saying that Zeus has laid on her and Alex-
andros an evil doom, "that we may be hereafter a theme of song for men to
come." But when we are simply told that Zeus "ensorcelled the mind of the
Achaeans," so that they fought badly, no consideration of persons comes
into play; still less in the general statement that "the gods can make the most
sensible man senseless and bring the feeble-minded to good sense." And
what, for example, of Glaucus, whose understanding Zeus took away, so
that he did what Greeks almost never do—accepted a bad bargain, by
swopping gold armour for bronze? Or what of Automedon, whose folly in
attempting to double the parts of charioteer and spearman led a friend to ask
him "which of the gods had put an unprofitable plan in his breast and taken
away his excellent understanding?" These two cases clearly have no connection with any deeper divine purpose; nor can there by any question of
retaining the hearers' sympathy, since no moral slur is involved.

At this point, however, the reader may naturally ask whether we are
dealing with anything more than a *façon de parler*. Does the poet mean
anything more than that Glaucus was a fool to make the bargain he did? Did
Automedon's friend mean anything more than "What the dickens prompted you to behave like that?" Perhaps not. The hexameter formulae which
were the stock-in-trade of the old poets lent themselves easily to the sort of
semasiological degeneration which ends by creating a *façon de parler*. And
we may note that neither the Glaucus episode nor the futile *aristeia* of
Automedon is integral to the plot even of an "expanded" *Iliad*: they may
well be additions by a later hand. Our aim, however, is to understand the
original experience which lies at the root of such stereotyped formulae—for
even a *façon de parler* must have an origin. It may help us to do so if we look
a little more closely at the nature of *atē* and of the agencies to which Agamemnon ascribes it, and then glance at some other sorts of statement which
the epic poets make about the sources of human behaviour.

There are a number of passages in Homer in which unwise and unaccountable conduct is attributed to *atē,* or described by the cognate verb
aasasthai, without explicit reference to divine intervention. But *atē* in Homer
is not itself a personal agent: the two passages which speak of *atē* in personal
terms, book 9, lines 505ff. and book 19, lines 91ff., are transparent pieces of
allegory. Nor does the word ever, at any rate in the *Iliad,* mean objective
disasters, as it so commonly does in tragedy. Always, or practically always,
atē is a state of mind—a temporary clouding or bewildering of the normal
consciousness. It is, in fact, a partial and temporary insanity; and, like all
insanity, it is ascribed, not to physiological or psychological causes, but to

an external "daemonic" agency. In the *Odyssey,* it is true, excessive consumption of wine is said to cause *atē*; the implication, however, is probably not that *atē* can be produced "naturally" but rather that wine has something supernatural or daemonic about it. Apart from this special case, the agents productive of *atē,* where they are specified, seem always to be supernatural beings, so we may class all instances of nonalcoholic *atē* in Homer under the head of what I propose to call "psychic intervention."

If we review them, we shall observe that *atē* is by no means necessarily either a synonym for, or a result of, wickedness. The assertion of Liddell and Scott that *atē* is "mostly sent as the punishment of guilty rashness" is quite untrue of Homer. The *atē* (here a sort of stunned bewilderment) which overtook Patroclus after Apollo had struck him might possibly be claimed as an instance, since Patroclus had rashly routed the Trojans *hyper aisan*; but earlier in the scene this rashness is itself ascribed to the will of Zeus and characterised by the verb *aasthē.* Again, the *atē* of one Agastrophus in straying too far from his chariot, and so getting himself killed, is not a "punishment" for rashness; the rashness is itself the *atē,* or a result of the *atē,* and it involves no discernible moral guilt—it is just an unaccountable error, like the bad bargain which Glaucus made. Again, Odysseus was neither guilty nor rash when he took a nap at an unfortunate moment, thus giving his companions a chance to slaughter the tabooed oxen. It was what we should call an accident; but for Homer, as for early thought in general, there is no such thing as accident—Odysseus knows that his nap was sent by the gods *eis atēn,* "to fool him." Such passages suggest that *atē* had originally no connection with guilt. The notion of *atē* as a punishment seems to be either a late development in Ionia or a late importation from outside: the only place in Homer where it is explicitly asserted is the unique *Litai* passage in *Iliad* 9, which suggests that it may possibly be a Mainland idea, taken over along with the Meleager story from an epic composed in the mother country.

A word next about the agencies to which *atē* is ascribed. Agamemnon cites, not one such agency, but three: Zeus and *moira* and the Erinys who walks in darkness (or, according to another and perhaps older reading, the Erinys who sucks blood). Of these, Zeus is the mythological agent whom the poet conceives as the prime mover in the affair: "the plan of Zeus was fulfilled." It is perhaps significant that (unless we make Apollo responsible for the *atē* of Patroclus) Zeus is the only individual Olympian who is credited with causing *atē* in the *Iliad* (hence *atē* is allegorically described as his eldest daughter). *Moira,* I think, is brought in because people spoke of any unaccountable personal disaster as part of their "portion" or "lot," meaning simply that they cannot understand why it happened, but since it has happened, evidently "it had to be." People still speak in that way, more especially of death, for which *mira* has in fact become a synonym in modern Greek, like *moros* in classical Greek. I am sure it is quite wrong to write *Moira* with a capital *M* here, as if it signified either a personal goddess who dictates to Zeus or a Cosmic Destiny like the Hellenistic *Heimarmenē*. As goddesses, *Moirai* are always plural, both in cult and in early literature, and with one doubtful exception they do not figure at all in the *Iliad*. The most we can say is that by treating his "portion" as an agent—by making it *do* something—Agamemnon is taking a first step towards personification. Again, by blaming his *moira* Agamemnon no more declares himself a systematic determinist than does the modern Greek peasant when he uses similar language. To ask whether Homer's people are determinists or libertarians is a fantastic anachronism: the question has never occurred to them, and if it were put to them, it would be very difficult to make them understand what it meant. What they do recognize is the distinction between normal actions and actions performed in a state of *atē*. Actions of the latter sort they can trace indifferently either to their *moira* or to the will of a god, according as they look at the matter from a subjective or an objective point of view. In the same way Patroclus attributes his death directly to the immediate agent, the man Euphorbus, and indirectly to the mythological agent, Apollo, but from a subjective standpoint to his bad *moira*. It is, as the psychologists say, "overdetermined."

On this analogy, the Erinys should be the immediate agent in Agamemnon's case. That she should figure at all in this context may well surprise those who think of an Erinys as essentially a spirit of vengeance, still more those who believe, with Rohde, that the Erinyes were originally the vengeful dead. But the passage does not stand alone. We read also in the *Odyssey* of "the heavy *atē* which the hard-hitting goddess Erinys laid on the understanding of Melampus." In neither place is there any question of revenge or punishment. The explanation is perhaps that the Erinys is the personal agent who ensures the fulfilment of a *moira*. That is why the Erinyes cut short the speech of Achilles' horses: it is not "according to *moira*" for horses to talk. That is why they would punish the sun, according to Heraclitus, if the sun should "transgress his measures" by exceeding the task assigned to him. Most probably, I think, the moral function of the Erinyes as ministers of vengeance derives from this primitive task of enforcing a *moira* which was at first morally neutral, or rather, contained by implication both an "ought" and a "must" which early thought did not clearly distinguish. So in Homer we find them enforcing the claims to status which arise from family or social relationship and are felt to be part of a person's *moira*: a parent, an elder brother, even a beggar, has something due to him as such, and can invoke "his" Erinyes to protect it. So too they are called upon to witness oaths; for the oath creates an assignment, a *moira*. The connection of Erinys with *moira* is still attested by Aeschylus, though the *moirai* have now become quasi-personal; and the Erinyes are still for Aeschylus dispensers of *atē*, although both they and it have been moralised. It rather looks as if the complex *moira*-Erinys-*atē* had deep roots, and might well be older than the ascription of *atē* to the agency of Zeus. In that connection it is worth recalling that Erinys and *aisa* (which is synonymous with *moira*) go back to what is perhaps the oldest known form of Hellenic speech, the Arcado-Cypriot dialect.

Here, for the present, let us leave *atē* and its associates, and consider briefly another kind of "psychic intervention" which is no less frequent in Homer, namely, the communication of power from god to man. In the *Iliad,* the typical case is the communication of *měnos* during a battle, as when Athena puts a triple portion of *menos* into the chest of her protégé Diomede, or Apollo puts *menos* into the *thumos* of the wounded Glaucus. This *menos* is not primarily physical strength; nor is it a permanent organ of mental life like *thymos* or *nŏŏs*. Rather it is, like *atē,* a state of mind. When a man feels *menos* in his chest, or "thrusting up pungently into his nostrils," he is conscious of a mysterious access of energy; the life in him is strong, and he is filled with a new confidence and eagerness. The connection of *menos* with the sphere of volition comes out clearly in the related words *menoinan,* "to be eager," and *dysmenēs,* "wishing ill." It is significant that often, though not always, a communication of *menos* comes as a response to prayer. But it is something much more spontaneous and instinctive than what we call "resolution"; animals can have it, and it is used by analogy to describe the devouring energy of fire. In man it is the vital energy, the "spunk," which is not always there at call, but comes and goes mysteriously and (as we should say) capriciously. But to Homer it is not caprice: it is the act of a god, who "increases or diminishes at will a man's *arĕtē* (that is to say, his potency as a fighter)." Sometimes, indeed, the *menos* can be roused by verbal exhortation; at other times its onset can only be explained by saying that a god has "breathed it into" the hero, or "put it in his chest," or, as we read in one place, transmitted it by contact, through a staff.

I think we should not dismiss these statements as "poetic invention" or "divine machinery." No doubt the particular instances are often invented by the poet for the convenience of his plot; and certainly the psychic intervention is sometimes linked with a physical one, or with a scene on Olympus. But we can be pretty sure that the underlying idea was not invented by any poet, and that it is older than the conception of anthropomorphic gods physically and visibly taking part in a battle. The temporary possession of a heightened *menos* is, like *atē,* an abnormal state which demands a supernormal explanation. Homer's men can recognise its onset, which is marked by a peculiar sensation in the limbs. "My feet beneath and hands above feel eager," says one recipient of the power; that is because, as the poet tells us, the god has made them nimble. This sensation, which is here shared by a second recipient, confirms for them the divine origin of the *menos.* It is an abnormal experience. And men in a condition of divinely heightened *menos* behave to some extent abnormally. They can perform the most difficult feats with ease: that is a traditional mark of divine power. They can even, like Diomede, fight with impunity against gods— an action which to men in their normal state is excessively dangerous. They are in fact for the time being rather more, or perhaps rather less, than human. Men who have received a communication of *menos* are several times compared to ravening lions; but the most striking description of the state is in book 15, where Hector goes berserk, he foams at the mouth, and his eyes glow. From such cases it is only a step to the idea of actual possession (*daimonan*); but it is a step which Homer does not take. He does say of Hector that after he had put on Achilles' armour "Ares entered into him and his limbs were filled with courage and strength"; but Ares here is hardly more than a synonym for the martial spirit, and the communication of power is produced by the will of Zeus, assisted perhaps by the divine armour. Gods do of course for purposes of disguise assume the shape and appearance of individual human beings; but that is a different belief. Gods may appear at times in human form, men may share at times in the divine attribute of power, but in Homer there is nevertheless no real blurring of the sharp line which separates humanity from deity.

In the *Odyssey,* which is less exclusively concerned with fighting, the communication of power takes other forms. The poet of the "Telemachy" imitates the *Iliad* by making Athena put *menos* into Telemachus; but here the *menos* is the *moral* courage which will enable the boy to face the overbearing suitors. That is literary adaptation. Older and more authentic is the repeated claim that minstrels derive their creative power from God. "I am self-taught," says Phemius; "it was a god who implanted all sorts of lays in my mind." The two parts of his statement are not felt as contradictory: he means, I think, that he has not memorised the lays of other minstrels, but is a creative poet who relies on the hexameter phrases welling up spontaneously as he needs them out of some unknown and uncontrollable depth; he sings "out of the gods," as the best minstrels always do. . . .

But the most characteristic feature of the *Odyssey* is the way in which its personages ascribe all sorts of mental (as well as physical) events to the intervention of a nameless and indeterminate daemon or "god" or "gods." These vaguely conceived beings can inspire courage at a crisis or take away a man's understanding, just as gods do in the *Iliad*. But they are also credited with a wide range of what may be called loosely "monitions." Whenever someone has a particularly brilliant or a particularly foolish idea; when he suddenly recognises another person's identity or sees in a flash the meaning of an omen; when he remembers what he might well have forgotten or forgets what he should have remembered, he or someone else will see in it, if we are to take the words literally, a psychic intervention by one of these anonymous supernatural beings. Doubtless they do not always expect to be taken literally: Odysseus, for example, is hardly serious in ascribing to the machinations of a daemon the fact that he went out without his cloak on a cold night. But we are not dealing simply with an "epic convention." For it is the poet's characters who talk like this, and not the poet: his own convention is quite other—he operates, like the author of the *Iliad,* with clear-cut anthropomorphic gods such as Athena and Poseidon, not with anonymous daemons. If he has made his characters employ a different convention, he has presumably done so because that is how people did in fact talk: he is being "realistic."

And indeed that is how we should expect people to talk who believed (or whose ancestors had believed) in daily and hourly monitions. The recognition, the insight, the memory, the brilliant or perverse idea, have this in common, that they come suddenly, as we say, "into a man's head." Often he is conscious of no observation or reasoning which has led up to them. But in that case, how can he call them "his"? A moment ago they were not in his mind; now they are there. Something has put them there, and that something is other than himself. More than this he does not know. So he speaks of it noncommittally as "the gods" or "some god," or more often (especially when its prompting has turned out to be bad) as a daemon. And by analogy he applies the same explanation to the ideas and actions of other people when he finds them difficult to understand or out of character. A good example is Antinous's speech in *Odyssey* 2, where, after praising Penelope's exceptional intelligence and propriety, he goes on to say that her idea of refusing to remarry is not at all proper, and concludes that "the gods are putting it into her chest." Similarly, when Telemachus for the first time speaks out boldly against the suitors, Antinous infers, not without irony, that "the gods are teaching him to talk big." His teacher is in fact Athena, as the poet and the reader know; but Antinous is not to know that, so he says "the gods."

A similar distinction between what the speaker knows and what the poet knows may be observed in some places in the *Iliad*. When Teucer's bowstring breaks, he cries out with a shudder of fear that a daemon is thwarting him; but it was in fact Zeus who broke it, as the poet has just told us. It has been suggested that in such passages the poet's point of view is the older: that he still makes use of the "Mycenaean" divine machinery, while his characters ignore it and use vaguer language like the poet's Ionian contemporaries, who (it is asserted) were losing their faith in the old anthropomorphic gods. In my view, as we shall see in a moment, this is almost an exact reversal of the real relationship. And it is anyhow clear that Teucer's vagueness has nothing to do with scepticism: it is the simple result of ignorance. By using the word *daemon* he "expresses the fact that a higher power has made something happen," and this fact is all he knows. As Ehnmark has pointed out, similar vague language in reference to the supernatural was commonly used by Greeks at all periods, not out of scepticism, but simply because they could not identify the particular god concerned. It is also commonly used by primitive peoples, whether for the same reason or because they lack the idea of personal gods. That its use by the Greeks is very old is shown by the high antiquity of the adjective *daemŏnios*. That word must originally have meant "acting at the monition of a daemon"; but already in the *Iliad* its primitive sense has so far faded that Zeus can apply it to Hera. A verbal coinage so defaced has clearly been in circulation for a long time.

We have now surveyed, in such a cursory manner as time permits, the commonest types of psychic intervention in Homer. We may sum up the result by saying that all departures from normal human behaviour whose causes are not immediately perceived, whether by the subjects' own consciousness or by the observation of others, are ascribed to a supernatural agency, just as is any departure from the normal behaviour of the weather or the normal behaviour of a bowstring. This finding will not surprise the nonclassical anthropologist: he will at once produce copious parallels from Borneo or Central Africa. But it is surely odd to find this belief, this sense of constant daily dependence on the supernatural, firmly embedded in poems supposedly so "irreligious" as the *Iliad* and the *Odyssey*. And we may also ask ourselves why a people so civilised, clear-headed, and rational as the Ionians did not eliminate from their national epics these links with Borneo and the primitive past, just as they eliminated fear of the dead, fear of pollution, and other primitive terrors which must originally have played a part in the saga. I doubt if the early literature of any other European people—even my own superstitious countrymen, the Irish—postulates supernatural interference in human behaviour with such frequency or over so wide a field.

Nilsson is, I think, the first scholar who has seriously tried to find an explanation of all this in terms of psychology. In a paper published in 1924, which has now become classical, he contended that Homeric heroes are peculiarly subject to rapid and violent changes of mood: they suffer, he says, from mental instability. And he goes on to point out that even today a person of this temperament is apt, when his mood changes, to look back with horror on what he has just done, and exclaim, "I didn't really mean to do that!"—from which it is a short step to saying, "It wasn't really I who did it." "His own behaviour," says Nilsson, "has become alien to him. He cannot understand it. It is for him no part of his Ego." This is a perfectly true observation, and its relevance to some of the phenomena we have been considering cannot, I think, be doubted. Nilsson is also, I believe, right in holding that experiences of this sort played a part—along with other elements, such as the Minoan tradition of protecting goddesses—in building up that machinery of *physical* intervention to which Homer resorts so constantly and, to our thinking, often so superfluously. We find it superfluous because the divine machinery seems to us in many cases to do no more than duplicate a natural psychological causation. But ought we not perhaps to say rather that the divine machinery "duplicates" a psychic intervention— that is, presents it in a concrete pictorial form? This was not superfluous; for only in this way could it be made vivid to the imagination of the hearers. The Homeric poets were without the refinements of language which would have been needed to "put across" adequately a purely psychological miracle. What more natural than that they should first supplement, and later replace, an old unexciting threadbare formula like *menos embale thumōi* by making the god appear as a physical presence and exhort his favourite with the spoken word? How much more vivid than a mere inward monition is the famous scene in *Iliad* 1 where Athena plucks Achilles by the hair and warns him not to strike Agamemnon! But she is visible to Achilles alone: "none of the others saw her." That is a plain hint that she is the projection, the pictorial expression, of an inward monition—a monition which Achilles might have described by such a vague phrase as *enepneuse phresi daimōn*. And I suggest that in general the inward monition, or the sudden unaccountable feeling of power, or the sudden unaccountable loss of judgement, is the germ out of which the divine machinery developed.

One result of transposing the event from the interior to the external world is that the vagueness is eliminated: the indeterminate daemon has to be made concrete as some particular personal god. In *Iliad* 1 he becomes Athena, the goddess of good counsel. But that was a matter for the poet's choice. And through a multitude of such choices the poets must gradually have built up the personalities of their gods, "distinguishing," as Herodotus says, "their offices and skills, and fixing their physical appearance." The poets did not, of course, invent the gods (nor does Herodotus say so): Athena, for example, had been, as we now have reason to believe, a Minoan house-goddess. But the poets bestowed upon them personality—and thereby, as Nilsson says, made it impossible for Greece to lapse into the magical type of religion which prevailed among her Oriental neighbours.

Some, however, may be disposed to challenge the assertion on which, for Nilsson, all this construction rests. *Are* Homer's people exceptionally unstable, as compared with the characters in other early epics? The evidence adduced by Nilsson is rather slight. They come to blows on small provocation; but so do Norse and Irish heroes. Hector on one occasion goes berserk; but Norse heroes do so much oftener. Homeric men weep in a more uninhibited manner than Swedes or Englishmen; but so do all the Mediterranean peoples to this day. We may grant that Agamemnon and Achilles are passionate, excitable men (the story requires that they should be). But are not Odysseus and Ajax in their several ways proverbial types of steady endurance, as is Penelope of female constancy? Yet these stable characters are not more exempt than others from psychic intervention. I should hesitate on the whole to press this point of Nilsson's, and should prefer instead to connect Homeric man's belief in psychic intervention with two other peculiarities which do unquestionably belong to the culture described by Homer.

The first is a negative peculiarity: Homeric man has no unified concept of what we call "soul" or "personality" (a fact to whose implications Bruno Snell has lately called particular attention). It is well known that Homer appears to credit man with a *psyche* only after death, or when he is in the act of fainting or dying or is threatened with death: the only recorded function of the *psyche* in relation to the living man is to leave him. Nor has Homer any other word for the living personality. The *thymos* may once have been a primitive "breath-soul" or "life-soul"; but in Homer it is neither the soul nor (as in Plato) a "part of the soul." It may be defined, roughly and generally, as the organ of feeling. But it enjoys an independence which the word "organ" does not suggest to us, influenced as we are by the later concepts of "organism" and "organic unity." A man's *thymos* tells him that he must now eat or drink or slay an enemy, it advises him on his course of action, it puts words into his mouth. He can converse with it, or with his "heart" or his "belly," almost as man to man. Sometimes he scolds these detached entities; usually he takes their advice, but he may also reject it and act as Zeus does on one occasion, "without the consent of his *thymos*." In the latter case, we should say, like Plato, that the man had controlled *himself*. But for Homeric man the *thymos* tends not to be felt as part of the self: it commonly appears as an independent inner voice. A man may even hear two such voices, as when Odysseus "plans in his *thymos*" to kill the Cyclops forthwith, but a second voice (*heteros thymos*) restrains him. This habit of (as we should say) "objectifying emotional drives," treating them as not-self, must have opened the door wide to the religious idea of psychic intervention, which is often said to operate, not directly on the man himself, but on his *thymos* or on its physical seat, his chest or midriff. We see the connection very clearly in Diomedes' remark that Achilles will fight "when the *thymos* in his chest tells him to *and* a god rouses him" (overdetermination again).

A second peculiarity, which seems to be closely related to the first, must have worked in the same direction. This is the habit of explaining character or behaviour in terms of knowledge. The most familiar instance is the very wide use of the verb *oida*, "I know," with a neuter plural object to express not only the possession of technical skill but also what we should call moral character or personal feelings: Achilles "knows wild things, like a lion," Polyphemus "knows lawless things," Nestor and Agamemnon "know friendly things to each other." This is not merely a Homeric "idiom": a similar transposition of feeling into intellectual terms is implied when we are told that Achilles has "a merciless *understanding*," or that the Trojans "*remembered* flight and *forgot* resistance." This intellectualist approach to the explanation of behaviour set a lasting stamp on the Greek mind: the so-called Socratic paradoxes, that "virtue is knowledge," and that "no one does wrong on purpose," were no novelties, but an explicit generalised formulation of what had long been an ingrained habit of thought. Such a habit of thought must have encouraged the belief in psychic intervention. If character is knowledge, what is not knowledge is not part of the character, but comes to a man from outside. When he acts in a manner contrary to the system of conscious dispositions which he is said to "know," his action is not properly his own, but has been dictated to him. In other words, unsystematised, nonrational impulses, and the acts resulting from them, tend to be excluded from the self and ascribed to an alien origin.

Evidently this is especially likely to happen when the acts in question are such as to cause acute shame to their author. We know how in our own society unbearable feelings of guilt are got rid of by "projecting" them in phantasy on to someone else. And we may guess that the notion of *atē* served a similar purpose for Homeric man by enabling him in all good faith to project on to an external power his unbearable feelings of shame. I say "shame" and not "guilt," for certain American anthropologists have lately taught us to distinguish "shame-cultures" from "guilt-cultures," and the society described by Homer clearly falls into the former class. Homeric man's highest good is not the enjoyment of a quiet conscience, but the enjoyment of *timē*, public esteem: "Why should I fight," asks Achilles, "if the good fighter receives no more *timē* than the bad?" And the strongest moral force which Homeric man knows is not the fear of god, but respect for public opinion, *aidōs*: *aideomai Trōas* says Hector at the crisis of his fate, and goes with open eyes to his death. The situation to which the notion of *atē* is a response arose not merely from the impulsiveness of Homeric man, but from the tension between individual impulse and the pressure of social conformity characteristic of a shame-culture. In such a society, anything which exposes a man to the contempt or ridicule of his fellows, which causes him to "lose face," is felt as unbearable. That perhaps explains how not only cases of moral failure, like Agamemnon's loss of self-control, but such things as the bad bargain of Glaucus, or Automedon's disregard of proper tactics, came to be "projected" on to a divine agency. On the other hand, it was the gradually growing sense of guilt, characteristic of a later age, which transformed *atē* into a punishment, the Erinyes into ministers of vengeance, and Zeus into an embodiment of cosmic justice. . . .

What I have thus far tried to do is to show, by examining one particular type of religious experience, that behind the term "Homeric religion" there lies something more than an artificial machinery of seriocomic gods and goddesses, and that we shall do it less than justice if we dismiss it as an agreeable interlude of lighthearted buffoonery between the presumed pro-fundities of an Aegean Earth-religion about which we know little, and those of an "early Orphic movement" about which we know even less.

Homeric Character
and the Tradition

Cedric H. Whitman

The developed form of Homeric epic differs radically, as was stated earlier, not only from the primitive saga, but even from the most sophisticated evolvements of oral poetry found anywhere. The preferences of Augustanism, periodically recurrent, have created a tendency to see in Homer a vigorous and effective, but primitive art. Such an idea, however, confuses subject matter with treatment. Homer's tales are old, and there is savagery in them. They are not "expurgated," but they are reconceived, and the Homeric reconception depends on as self-conscious an artistry as is to be found in literature. The poet's predecessors, answering as they could the changing demands of Greek taste, doubtless account for something, but it is imponderable. We must deal with Homer as we find him, reckoning with oral methods both in their limitations and their opportunities; and what we find is highly sophisticated, subtle, and contrived. The contents, like the contents of Geometric art, have an archaic look at times; but the touch is controlled, the intention steady, and the design ever present. If the festivals and what they implied for Greek culture in the eighth century provided the setting and conditions for such art, the nature of the art and its motivation must be sought in the poems themselves.

For a poet whose language and whole artistic medium is bound by the fairly rigid rules of an age-old tradition, the problem of originality is in great part one of formal mastery. But it also lies in the intellectual or intuitive penetration of the themes and character shapes which constitute the heroic

From *Homer and the Heroic Tradition*. © 1958 by the President and Fellows of Harvard College. Harvard University Press, 1958.

typology. Parallels are not far to seek in early epic literature for the various kinds of valor represented by Homer. Everywhere can be found, reshaped according to shifting cultural standards, the ideal hero, *chevalier sans peur et sans reproche,* the crafty hero, the boaster, the grim and aging warrior, the slightly buffoonish hero, the aged king, the warrior virgin, the wise counselor, or the young reckless fighter. Action also falls into types: the typical siege, the brilliant trick, the hand-to-hand duel, imprisonment and release of a famous warrior, disappearance, and return. Such blueprints of character and action lie in the storehouse of Western culture, heavy with poetic implications. In selecting as the core of the *Iliad* the pattern of the hero who retires from the war, Homer probably did nothing extraordinary. The type surely existed, as the tale of Meleager shows. But to build this theme into a study of heroic self-searching and the dark night of the soul was creativity in the highest sense, and a far cry from those glimpses of an old Achaean rough-and-tumble which occasionally peer through the texture of Homer's work. Homer's genius is like a shuttle drawing the warp of profound self-consciousness across the woof of old, half primitive material, from the time when heroism meant chiefly physical prowess, murderous dexterity, colossal self-assertion. Yet it is also perhaps part of essential human equipment that the germs of a corrective to this self-assertion are not wholly lacking among the original types themselves. The hero who retires out of wounded honor, though he may not achieve the stature of Achilles, must nevertheless be in some degree a man of complex sensibility. There is an interesting brief episode in one of the Serbian epics which relates how one hero went out to slay a famous marauder; he accomplished his task, but then was stricken with remorse for having slain one better than himself, and disappeared forever into a cave. In the Arthurian legend, it will be remembered, Lancelot has periods of madness, when he is helpless, and Orlando too went mad. The consciousness of despair amid greatness and success was probably not originally the most popular theme for epic singing, but in Homer's hands, it grew to overshadow all else, and formulated, for the first time that we know of, the primal shape of tragedy.

The problem of Homer's originality, raised earlier, is actually simplified rather than obscured by the oral theory. The only function denied Homer by the nature of his medium was, for the most part, novelty of phrase. All the larger aspects of his poetry were his own to form, character, structure, imagistic economy, and above all, point. It has actually been suggested that Hector and Patroclus are his own inventions. It cannot, of course, be proved whether they are or not, and the assumption seems a little unlikely. On the other hand, it is also unnecessary, for beyond question

Homer has shaped these two figures, along with all his others, to a purpose wholly his own; there is a strong probability that whatever Hector and Patroclus were earlier, in Homer they have become something new, and comprehensible only as parts of the *Iliad*. The careful and consistent identification of Hector with Troy itself, especially in the Andromache scene and the scene where his death symbolizes the fall of the city, can have found its motivation only in a poem which aimed at drawing the significance of the whole epic tradition about Troy into the framework of a single dramatic action. So too, Patroclus, whether created from nothing or from a figure already existent, could never have attained his complex character outside a poem which required him to substitute for the dread Achilles on the battlefield, and at the same time to be the embodiment of gentleness and friendship.

Similar observations could be made about practically all the characters in the *Iliad*. One cannot, for instance, imagine that Agamemnon always appeared in epic tradition as he does in Homer. The great king of Mycenae must have been represented as noble, at least at his own court. But Homer has handled him with the most subtle irony, as a foil to Achilles, using all his traditional eminence as a means of diminishing the man. Early in the poem, Nestor points the issue nicely, when he attempts to bring Achilles into reconcilement with the king:

> Do not you, Achilles, set your will at strife with a king,
> Hostile, for never a scepter-bearing king, to whom Zeus gives
> Glory, has stood in equal honor with other men
> If you are the mightier, and a goddess was your mother,
> Yet he is greater, for he rules over more men.
>
> (bk. 1, ll. 277–81)

Nestor has stated the case precisely as Achilles will not allow it. To the semidivine hero, the mere fact of ruling over more men does not constitute greatness, and as for glory from Zeus, Achilles will prove by example which of them has more. The contest between Achilles and Agamemnon becomes from the outset a contest between internal and external value, a little after the manner of Sophocles' last play, though of course more diffused. It is interesting to observe, for instance, that the dress and general appearance of Agamemnon are obsequiously described three times, besides lesser mentions, and always in strictly concrete and factual terms. The dress of Achilles is never described, except when he puts on the miraculous armor of Hephaestus. His appearance is never described at all, though it is constantly reckoned with in imagery. Agamemnon's whole psychology is bound and limited by his own material greatness. The quarrel in the first place arises from his sense of outrage that he will be the only one of the Achaeans without a prize, if he should give Chryseis back to her father. His demand for a substitute girl, who will be "just as good," further limns his emphasis on the cash value of things, and contrasts subtly with Achilles' statement that he himself really loves Briseis. The king's proffered amends in the ninth book are of similar kind: cities, bronze, gold, tripods, women, a state-marriage. Achilles' refusal of them at first and his disinterest when they are finally delivered are both symptoms of his insistence on the spirit. In what a different mood does he accept Priam's ransom for Hector, together with Priam himself! And as if to give the whole issue a final touch, at the end of the funeral games for Patroclus, Homer makes Achilles award the great king a prize for spear-throwing—an honorary token, for which he has not even competed; twice earlier, Achilles has stated that Agamemnon never earned any of the honors and rewards which he received.

In some of Agamemnon's scenes, one may recognize motifs which doubtless are traditional. His discouragement and proposal to go home may well be a stock attitude for the leader of a host under certain circumstances. But Homer has used the theme to underline certain phases of the action and to illustrate the character of the king. It occurs three times, twice in identical words. His first speech in the assembly of book 2 is a falsehood contrived to test the spirit of the army, and, more important, to test the validity of his dream by stating the opposite of what he hopes and believes to be true, to see if the gods will intervene:

> O friends, heroes, Danaoi, comrades of Ares,
> Zeus son of Cronos has mightily caught me in heavy doom,
> Wretch, who promised first, and nodded me acquiescence,
> I should sack Ilion, well-walled city, and turn home;
> Vile deceit he devised, and now as it is, he bids me
> Go ill-famed to Argos, when I have lost many soldiers.
> Likely such, I suppose, was the pleasure of the almighty
> Zeus, who indeed has shattered the crowns of many a city,
> Yes, and will shatter still; for his power is supreme.
>
> (bk. 2, ll. 110–18)

It can be no casual coincidence that, weeping like a dark-watered spring, Agamemnon repeats this speech word for word in the night council after the first day's defeat. He had spoken more truly than he knew; now that the truth is out, he is ready to propitiate Achilles. The latter's answer is, of course, a counterproposal that he himself go home, not out of fear of failure, but out of resentment at a breach of mutual respect among warriors. Diomedes' rebuke to Agamemnon's flagging courage at this point is respectful but firm. That of Odysseus, when Agamemnon for the third time proposes flight, is plainly contemptuous. In these passages, a traditional motif, familiar for the hard-pressed leader of a host, has been turned and deployed to its full psychological worth.

So too with the *aristeia* of Agamemnon, which initiates the Great Battle. On the surface, but only on the surface, this series of exploits resembles all the others. The arming of the central figure, violent death on the field, comparisons to fierce animals, and the flight of the enemy are all familiar elements. But every Homeric *aristeia* is a character sketch, and in this we see another side of Agamemnon. The arming scene is greatly inflated to include the description of the magnificent breastplate, gift of Cinyras of Cyprus; the shield wears not the supernal, cosmic signals of Achilles' shield, but a terrible-faced Gorgon, as motto for what is to come. Homer's battles are full of images of pity and terror, but in this scene there is a singular concentration of them. Here all is intensely grim. Bianor is speared through the brain, and he and his companions stripped and left naked on the field. Two sons of Priam follow—Isus and Antiphus, the latter once a captive of Achilles who spared him for ransom; Agamemnon drives his sword into his ear, and is thereupon compared to a lion crunching with his strong teeth the helpless children of a deer. One is reminded of the Thyestean banquet, and the eating of Pelops. Next come Pisander and Hippolochus, who sue for mercy; they are refused, on the ground that their father had advised against giving Helen back to Menelaus. Agamemnon cuts off the head and hands of Hippolochus, and hurls the head "like a quoit" through the host. The flight and rally of the Trojans by the city gates leads to another image of Agamemnon "covered with gore," and a comparison again to a lion, this time frightening a herd of cows, slaying one, breaking its neck, and licking the blood and entrails. At this point, Zeus begins to turn the tide in favor of the Trojans, but Agamemnon slays one more man before he is himself wounded. Iphidamas, son of Antenor, young and newly married, rushes at Agamemnon, and is slashed in the neck:

> Thus he fell, and slept the brazen sleep,
> Pitiable, helping the citizens, far from the modest bride
> He wooed, whose grace he saw not, though he gave much.
> (bk. 11, ll. 241–43)

Herewith the sequence of terrible and sorry images which surround Agamemnon reaches a climax. The brother of Iphidamas tries to rescue the body; he wounds Agamemnon, but is himself slain and beheaded. Then Homer adds a rarity: he describes the pain of Agamemnon's wound. External symptoms of pain—writhing, swooning, shrieking—often appear. But here, almost with satisfaction, the poet says that the keen pangs assailed the king's spirit like the pains of childbirth, and with this grotesque conceit, the exploits of Agamemnon end. Unlike any other *aristeia,* this one achieves scarcely even a degree of victory, but only the first ironical phase of the long defeat which brings honor to Achilles.

However the words and formulae of this passage are epic stock in trade, the circumstances and description attending the wounding of Agamemnon are carefully designed somehow to be in character. Odysseus and Diomedes are also presently wounded, and reveal themselves similarly. Odysseus slays by trickery the man who has scathed him, and then, still fighting like a lion beset by jackals, prudently retreats under the shield of Ajax. Diomedes, shot through the foot by Paris, high-heartedly taunts his victor with cowardice, and says he does not care about this wound, any more than if a woman or a brainless child had hit him. The surprising simile of the birth-pangs lends an odd air to the case of Agamemnon; as if the Hellenic intuition of *nemesis* found it appropriate for this savage and merciless slayer, who eats the helpless children of deer, to balance his heritage of child-eating with the pains of childbearing.

The refusal of mercy, together with the motives implied, also prompts comparison with other passages. Achilles, in his *aristeia,* refuses the appeal of Lycaon; but the speech he makes says simply that death is the law of the world, that the good and the bad all die, himself included, and there is actually no escape; calling Lycaon "friend," as if by the bond of mutual mortality, he slays him. Such knowledgeable passion as this is not the fruit of a spite which remembers the hostile action of the victim's father. Whereas to Achilles, Lycaon is in some large sense a friend, to Agamemnon, the suppliants before him are simply enemies. The enemy deserves no quarter, and far from giving it himself, Agamemnon will not even allow Menelaus to give it. "Have they benefited your house?" he asks. "Let not one escape death at our hands," adding characteristically, not even the boy the mother carries in her womb." When Achilles wills death to all the Trojans, he wills it for all the Greeks too, except himself and Patroclus, in a speech which will demand attention later, but the contrast in the treatment of a theme is evident.

Again, the scepter of the king of Mycenae was the symbol of the mightiest royal power in Greece. Homer describes it famously—forged by Hephaestus, given by Zeus, descended through Pelops, Atreus, and Thyestes to Agamemnon. Yet this magnificent adjunct, so carefully brought before our eyes, is involved in some disillusioning contexts. Leaning on it, Agamemnon makes his deceitful proposal to return home and give up the war. Odysseus, inspired by Athena, runs to Agamemnon and receives from him the "ancestral, imperishable scepter" as a badge of vicarious authority. With gentle words he restrains the leaders, but the common folk he rounds up like a herd, using the scepter physically as a goad. When the host is reassembled, the ugly and lowborn Thersites rises and rails at Agamemnon; his words echo those of Achilles, in the previous book, as he accuses the king of greed and unfairness, and by a skillful turn he ends his harangue with a line which Achilles himself had used to the effect that such a king as Agamemnon must rule over "good-for-nothings," or he would presently be murdered. Few things are more subtle in the *Iliad* than the way in which this "good-for-nothing," the social and physical antitype of Achilles, reiterates the resentment of the hero: the theme of the entire second book is Delusion, and truth can appear only in the mouth of a Thersites. He is silenced by Odysseus, with a violent blow of the lordly scepter, while the other soldiers, unhappy as they are, laugh at him. What is Homer saying through these scepter-passages, except that Agamemnon, himself deceived by Zeus, is deceiving and bullying his people into disaster? The scepter is no mere ornament; it enters into the actions of its owner, as the agent of power misled and misused. How differently Achilles treats the scepter which he holds when he makes his tense and furious oath:

> Yea, by this scepter, which never again shall put forth
> Leaves and branches, now it has left its stump in the mountains,
> Nor shall it bloom; for the bronze has lopped it round,
> Leaves and bark, and the sons of Achaeans bear it,
> Justice-deliverers, in their palms, who draw from Zeus
> Judgments; here, hark you, shall be a great oath:
> Yearning for Achilles shall surely come to the sons of Achaeans,
> All . . .
>
> . . . .
>
> So spoke the son of Peleus, and hurled to earth the scepter
> Studded with golden nails, and himself sat down.

There is no need to labor the contrast between the scepter of kingly violence, and the lopped and leafless scepter which is a symbol of finality, hurled in contempt on the ground in token of Achilles' defiance of external authority.

In scene after scene, the character of Agamemnon, which one might a priori expect to be massive and imposing, is undercut with consistency throughout the poem. Yet the touch is everywhere light; and Agamemnon is allowed to gain sympathy, if not respect. His very weakness, the helpless way he stumbles against his own limits and infinite pretensions, win him some measure of compassion. He usually offends those whom he addresses, except his immediate henchmen, who suppress their feelings. A little scene with Teucer is most characteristic; Teucer is doing well in battle, and wins Agamemnon's praise:

> If ever Zeus the aegis-holder and Athena grant me
> To spoil the well-founded citadel of Troy,
> Into your hand I will put a token of honor,
> First—after myself.
>
> (bk. 8, ll. 287–89)

Teucer impudently answers, "Why do you spur me on when I am working on my own account?" and Agamemnon vanishes for the rest of the book. One of his best features is perhaps his solicitous care for Menelaus, yet this devotion is wholly unlike the high-hearted friendship of Diomedes and Sthenelus, the passionate unity of Achilles and Patroclus, or the studious and admiring love of Nestor for the gallant younger men. Agamemnon fusses over Menelaus and worries about him. When Menelaus is grazed by an arrow, Agamemnon's lament over the wound is almost hysterical. No great warrior himself, Menelaus has a fine moment, when he rises to answer Hector's challenge, and hopes the rest of the Achaeans turn to "earth and water," for being so spiritless; but Agamemnon seizes him and makes him sit down in safety. His very solicitude betokens more fear than love, even as his prayer for the army's safety, by contrast with the famous prayer of Ajax for death under a clear sky, accents his timorous nature, insecure in itself and a fuse of alarm to others.

Homer's sense of character is always profound, but Agamemnon is a consummate masterpiece. There is no reason to believe that he was always drawn as Homer draws him; rather the opposite. As in the case of Patroclus and Hector, the man is envisioned within the framework of the total poem; his traditional kingly attributes, his primacy among peers, his position of marshaler of the spearmen, his personal exploits, and even his scepter, have all been used, but used with a difference, to establish him as the opposite of Achilles—the nadir, as Achilles is the zenith, of the heroic assumption. As Homer makes Agamemnon, he is a magnificently dressed incompetence, without spirit or spiritual concern; his dignity is marred by pretension; his munificence by greed, and his prowess by a savagery which is the product of a deep uncertainty and fear. Yet none of this is ever overtly stated. He is always the king, with honorifics ever present. If Thersites bawls at him, Nestor, that repository of courteous mores, instructs him. The mores must be kept by all except those able to transcend them. It is for Achilles to reveal their real transparency. If Homer had acted overtly in drawing the feebleness of Agamemnon, the *Iliad* would have been satire, not tragedy. It is part of the tragedy that Agamemnon never meets with full disgrace, or understands himself really at all.

Such individual elaborations upon the heroic norm, and in particular the difference of value so implied, must be in some part the consequence of molding the large epic out of the short epic song. From the first, the various famous figures must have been characterized by certain individual traits, some perhaps more than others; but there could have been little motive to represent their special relationship to the heroic heritage, their comparative individual interpretations of its meaning. Nobility, *arete,* a valuable composite of personal, social, and military features, was the assumption for all, and, though in different times and districts it would have presented varying aspects, the implicit cultural aspiration was universally accepted without definition. An individual hero would receive his due of admiration in terms appropriate to the people or city to which he belonged historically; if a singer thought well of an action which was narrated of some other warrior, he could, if it were not too specifically pinned to someone else, expropriate it for the character he had in hand. The generalized epithets which form units with the personal names illustrate well the fundamental unity of the heroic tradition. These epithets, "strong," "swift-footed," "good at the war-shout," "plume-crested," "bronze-clad," do, as Parry once wrote, adorn not individuals, but the whole of epic verse. They spring from a universally recognized ideal which in its early phase envelops character, rather than testing it or illuminating it. With the first attempt to weld the short tales of single exploits into a panorama of all the heroes, a new problem arises. The characters must either duplicate each other to the point of utter boredom, or their individual differences must begin to distinguish them. Once the latter process has begun, we are on our way toward that extraordinary roster of unforgettable individuals which Homer presents. His formulation is surely not the only one which ever could have been, though its self-completeness suggests as much. Any bard dealing with the amalgamation of epic traditions must have attempted something of the sort. But Homer's construction is the one which impressed the Greeks, and laid the basis for all subsequent conceptions of the figures of myth, both gods and heroes, as Herodotus says.

But the process of distinguishing the characters of tradition involved more than merely letting the inevitable happen. It meant building consciously upon rudimentary data; it involved a shift of interest from merely what happened (to the greater glory of somebody) to how and why it happened, to whom, and through the agency of what sort of man. In the *Iliad,* at least, the question even arises as to what is the greater glory, and to whom can it come. It is naive to think that Homer celebrates all his heroes equally simply because his epithets do. The keen principle of dramatic selection is constantly at work in his exploration of the meaning of heroism. In Homer, many are called to the heroic trial, but in the last analysis, only one is chosen. Others achieve a partial glorification, and some are even consigned to the muster, not of heroes, but of ruffians. Agamemnon's character, with its grievous shortcomings, is saved from ridicule by the mores and by the more important necessity of giving Achilles an adversary of weight and seriousness. Some lesser characters are not so fortunate. Ajax the son of Oileus, for instance, appears only in the Great Battle, sometimes as companion of his great namesake, and in the Games of Patroclus. In the Battle, his deeds, like those of Agamemnon, involve a special insulting violence. He hurls severed heads like balls, and murders his captives. When the Trojans momentarily break and flee before Poseidon at the end of book 14, Ajax is accorded the dubious distinction of being the best at overtaking and killing men who are running away. His only other appearances are a couple of indifferent slayings and the footrace with Odysseus and Antilochus in the Games. In this passage, Homer reserves the only low humor in the *Iliad* for Ajax; Athena makes him slip and fall headlong in the manure of the sacrificed cattle, and thus lose the race. Is it fanciful to see herein a foreshadowing of Athena's revenge on him for his rape of Cassandra in the sack of Troy, and the poet's contemptuous dismissal of him as a mere thug? As he picks himself up from the ordure, the Achaeans laugh at him, and the only other person laughed at in misfortune is Thersites. Whatever his reputation had been in his native Locris, in Homer he has become a sketch of mean violence, and Idomeneus's judgment, which seems to be also Homer's, adhered to him. In this figure, as in one or two others in the *Iliad,* where the hero is submerged in the fighter, one may see a reaction from the primitive admiration for a man who kills his enemy. Idomeneus, though he is drawn more sympathetically than the Locrian Ajax, is another such. He is represented as slightly aging, but still efficiently deadly on the battlefield, where, in book 13 particularly, he, with Poseidon, leads the counterattack. There is something noticeably grim about him, and also something coldly professional. In the midst of the battle he holds a long, cool discussion with his companion Meriones about spears and the proper behavior in battle and ambush. He knows his subject well, estimating the symptoms of cowardice with precision, and praising his friend's valor with unemotional approval. This is the only occasion on which Idomeneus is allowed to speak, except for battle speeches of encouragement or challenge; he never utters a word in council. He reveals himself as a fighter, one of the most dangerous, but as nothing else, and all his deeds, successful as they are, are buried in an atmosphere of complete indifference.

The spirit of the epic was traditionally that of praise, and it is not surprising that the less favorably drawn characters of the *Iliad* receive, on the whole, brief treatment, while those who demand admiration are given many lines. The exception is, of course, Agamemnon, for obvious reasons. Aside from Achilles, the men who really interest Homer are Ajax of Salamis, Diomedes, Hector, Nestor, and, in the next rank, Odysseus, Paris, Antilochus, Priam, Helen, Aeneas, and Menelaus. One may well ask why Homer gives so much attention to Ajax and Diomedes; national considerations could have had little to do with it, for Homer's audience was the international one of the festivals. The tradition, the tales themselves, can account for what was actually told, perhaps. But only the poet's total intention can explain the selection of what he tells, and in particular his developed portraits of Diomedes' dashing brilliance, and the sound magnificence of Ajax. Each has a special atmosphere; one thinks of Diomedes as always in rapid motion, of Ajax as immovably fixed to the earth, and these two contrasting images, which persist although Ajax does move and Diomedes can stand still, typify two aspects of heroism which Homer has chosen to embody in these two figures, motion and rest, action and endurance. These are real heroes, in the sense of what the tradition transmitted at its best, and they are normative, in a way, for that cultural aspiration which the tradition enshrined. Where Achilles is snared in all its tragic implications, Diomedes and Ajax fulfill the ideal with a kind of saving simplicity which renders them children beside Achilles, but children of an admirable and fine grain.

One of the pleasantest features of Diomedes' character is reflected in his relationship with Nestor. The latter's age and eminence render him the acknowledged guardian of the ideals, as socially conceived and accepted. Nestor remonstrates on occasion with Achilles, and almost constantly with Agamemnon, but for Diomedes he has only praise. In its simple outlines, the great tradition of the epic lives in Nestor; hence his approval of Diomedes stamps the latter as a type of proper behavior. It may well be that Homer invented this whole relationship quite purposefully, and built it, as usual, upon a slightly altered strand of tradition. In the *Aethiopis,* Nestor's son Antilochus loses his life rescuing his father from a maimed and tangled chariot on the battlefield, and there are those who believe that the scene in the eighth *Iliad,* where Nestor is rescued by Diomedes, is based on this scene. Certainly the episode preceded both poems, and was one of the traditional stories told of the gallant Antilochus, whom Achilles especially loved. In giving an identical action to Diomedes, Homer created a father-son relationship, which becomes quite outspoken in the Embassy, when Nestor, warming to a courageous speech of Diomedes, says:

> Son of Tydeus, verily brave are you in battle,
> Best also in council among all your equals in years;
> No one will blame your speech, of all the Achaeans,
> Nor will he contradict; yet you reach not the fullness of words.
> Well, you are young, indeed, and well might you be
>   my own son,
> Youngest of all my brood; you utter prudence
> Unto the Argive kings, for you have spoken in season.
>
> (bk. 9, ll. 53–59)

Nestor's only criticism is that Diomedes' speech was not long enough; he himself will make up the deficiency. The remark about Diomedes as Nestor's own son perhaps reveals Homer's consciousness of having transferred the rescue episode from Antilochus, and certainly characterizes Diomedes as the fully satisfactory offspring of the epic ideal. Diomedes subordinates himself to this ideal in every respect, and his contentment with it is subtly indicated in his cheerful obedience to all his superiors. When Agamemnon unjustly reproves him, he is shamefaced and silent, and when Nestor wakes him out of a sound sleep by kicking him, his irritation takes the form of an admiring compliment to the old man's indefatigable energy and zeal.

The longest book in the *Iliad* is the *aristeia* of Diomedes, a series of exploits surpassed in length and development only by the *aristeia* of Achilles himself, which stretches over four books (19–22). As the first and last *aristeiai* of the poem, they balance each other to a degree and prompt comparison. Right at the beginning, Diomedes in arms is compared to a star. The comparison of an armed hero to the star Sirius is doubtless traditional enough; and it has already been pointed out how Homer applies it also to Achilles, but with additional lines which make it, in his case, a bright but deadly star, a token of evil, a bringer of fever, which rises under the weight of the whole tragedy of Troy and of Achilles himself. Diomedes' star is simply bright, washed in the ocean; no extra vista of tragedy attends the work of Diomedes. His is the heroic pattern without thought, victory without implicit defeat.

A hero's display of valor offered a special opportunity for virtuosity, and Homer here has not missed his chance. Where the vigorous deeds of Patroclus and Achilles on the field sound the deepest and most central tones of the poem, those of Diomedes are a display for its own sake; yet many of the motifs are identical. A hero in action might often, we presume, struggle with a god. Patroclus is thrust back from the wall of Troy by Apollo three times before he yields, and the passage foreshadows Apollo's destruction of him later. Diomedes also makes three assaults on Apollo, who is defending Aeneas, and is similarly thrust back. But thereafter, Apollo retires to Pergamon, and sends Ares to quell Diomedes. This is a most telling difference, for Ares in the *Iliad* has always a certain grotesque buffoonery about him, and he is always defeated. Homer never allows the slightest indignity to approach Apollo, although he is on the Trojan side. But Ares is contemptible in all eyes, and Diomedes' victory over him, with Athena's help, is about comparable to his earlier victory over Aphrodite. Both of these triumphs are full of sound and fury, signifying, if anything, the inconsequence of what is done. Indeed, nothing is really done. Aside from motivating Hector's journey to Troy in the next book, Diomedes' *aristeia* has no effect on the war, and his enormous thunderings gradually fade away until he is wounded in book 11. Almost all the gods appear in the course of his actions, yet nowhere else in the *Iliad,* not even in the Theomachia, are the gods presented more simply as figures of fairy tale, bright adornments of a gay, victorious fantasy. Diomedes is early wounded by Pandarus, but is promptly and magically restored by Athena. The gods' miracles are never without some support in the realities of the situation, and one may say here, as Homer does, that "the arrow did not subdue him." Yet the cure is so quick, and the significance for the whole so slight, it seems almost as much a joke as the rapid cure of Aphrodite's wounded hand. Aeneas's wound is also hastily cured; that of Ares heals like curdling milk. Sarpedon's wound is more serious, but though it is not miraculously healed, it is forgotten. Wounds in this book do not count for much. The emphasis is on the joy of battle, with its romantic high-heartedness. Brilliant descriptions and handsome similes decorate the action, such as the vision of the Achaeans "dusty as winnowers," or standing in battle unmoved as clouds on a windless day. There are some fine inversions: blood drawn by an arrow spurts back like a javelin, and Diomedes, himself compared earlier to a flooding river, quails before Hector's counterattack like a man before a rushing river. To what a different climax the motif of man versus river comes in book 21! Here only the external appearances are consulted, and some of them are superb. The description of the arming of Hera and Athena and their journey to the field in a fiery chariot, their horses leaping at each bound as far as a man can see over the ocean, is a marvel of extended imaginative vividness.

Homer's method of characterization, as is well known, objectifies internal states into visible figures, often into gods. If the valor of Diomedes is objectified in the figures of Hera and Athena, yet there is a difference here too. In the case of the more weighted figures of the poem, especially Achilles, the gods' participation on the whole follows a motivation in the human sphere, as will be shown later. But Diomedes is instructed by Athena right at the start in what he is to do and he simply does it. As she cures his wound, she takes the "mist" from his eyes, so that he can recognize gods, if necessary, and warns him not to fight with any except Aphrodite. Obediently Diomedes goes and wounds Aphrodite. For a moment, he is carried away and tries to kill Aeneas in the arms of Apollo, but desists in time, and real conflict is avoided. The sight of Ares accompanying Hector causes him to retreat, until Athena rejoins him and assists him against the god. Diomedes stays well within the rules, and nothing that he does suggests a will to break the framework, or show himself too stubborn in the face of war's alternations of fortune. In book 8, when the lightning of Zeus drives back the Achaeans, Diomedes yields more reluctantly than the others; but there is nothing in his character that bears the gods along with him, or qualifies in any way the limits and realities which they represent. They play on him, not he on them. He is the product, not the creator, of the heroic assumption, and as such he can state, more clearly than anyone else on occasion, the norm of high valor, without reference to any embarrassing complexities. His performance in the horse race at the Games is a clean sweep to victory, and the poet turns away from it immediately to develop instead the revealing little scene of altercation between Antilochus and Menelaus. Diomedes is a success, and Homer throughout lets him pay the price of it.

Ajax of Salamis is a different matter. Constantly referred to as the greatest of the Achaeans after Achilles, he is nevertheless given no *aristeia,* and no scene of distinction which is his alone. Two stories in particular were traditional about Ajax: how he defended the corpse of Achilles and how he went mad and killed himself, after the loss of Achilles' arms to Odysseus. Homer narrates neither of these tales, though he seems to have both in mind. The wrestling match in book 23 with Odysseus doubtless prefigures the Judgment of the Arms. Ajax lifts Odysseus in the air, but the latter topples his opponent by trick. Odysseus cannot lift Ajax, but falls himself, dragging

Ajax down a second time. At this point, Achilles interferes and awards equal prizes; but enough has been said. The man of force has hit the ground twice, the man of guile only once, and the results of the Judgment of Arms are distinctly hinted. It has also been persuasively argued that the fight over Patroclus's body in book 17 is based on a poem about the defense of Achilles' body. This is probably in some sense true; yet the seventeenth book was known in antiquity as the *aristeia* of Menelaus, and reasonably, since here Menelaus, standing "like a mother cow over her first-born calf," fights off the attackers for some time before he is joined by Ajax, and even then, he is by no means eclipsed by the latter. The action of carrying a comrade's body out of a hot melee must have been stock in trade, and for its final accomplishment, it called for teamwork; someone must carry the corpse while others cover his retreat. In Homer's treatment, the idea of cooperation in battle becomes the dominant one for the whole section, transcending the more usual individualistic outlook of the heroes. Isolated at first, Menelaus is hesitant to face Hector, who seems god-inspired; but he reflects that with Ajax beside him he would fight even against a god. Two images of animals protecting young suggest the tenderer side of heroic brotherhood, called forth by the fall of the gentle Patroclus. In a singularly outspoken moment of fear, Ajax says simply that he is not so worried about the corpse of Patroclus as he is about his own head and that of Menelaus. Later, as they look about for someone to take the terrible news to Achilles, Antilochus is drawn in as a climax of the picture of struggling, sorrowful survivors. As he hears of Patroclus's death, Antilochus's eyes fill with tears and he is stricken dumb for a moment before he turns to take the news. Hitherto, we had heard nothing of any special love between Antilochus and Patroclus; but this is a book devoted to loyalties, the dependency of fellow soldiers on each other. As Antilochus leaves, it is remarked that his Pylians missed him, though frequently in the *Iliad* warriors leave the field for one purpose or another without any notice being taken of their departure. The sense of loss and of loyalty penetrates everywhere, even to the Trojan side. In an angry speech to Hector, Glaucus demands that he get the corpse of Patroclus to use in exchange for that of Sarpedon, which has fallen, as Glaucus thinks, into the hands of the enemy. Sarpedon's body had actually been spirited away, by Sleep and Death, to his home in Lycia, and the present passage has been pointed to as an inconsistency. But it is quite consistent with the book as a whole, with its peculiar concern with the comradeship and mutual obligation of allies. If this book was modeled on an old poem about Ajax's stout deeds over the corpse of Achilles, it has certainly developed into something else, something, indeed, quite consistent with Homer's view of Ajax elsewhere.

In the *Iliad,* the word for responsibility to others, and a sense of their importance to oneself, is *aidôs.* It is *aidôs* that keeps Hector in the forefront of his troops. For the greater part, the Homeric heroes fight for their own individual glory, but a few of them are further motivated by a feeling of duty. Menelaus, for instance, a peace-loving man, self-effacing to the point of being at times ineffectual, fights under the pressure of his personal loss, rather than for glory, and feels deeply the responsibility he owes to the Achaeans suffering in his cause. Antilochus also, traditionally the rescuer of his father, shows a friendly concern for Menelaus, who admires the young man's spirit. But more than any other figure on the Greek side, Ajax is the man of *aidôs.* Throughout the Great Battle, other heroes come and go, distinguishing themselves variously, though the most eminent are absent because of their wounds. But the poet keeps bringing Ajax in; he seems to go on forever, slowly beaten back, but steadily fighting without rest or haste, holding his post, and only changing it if some special danger threatens in another place. He is in his element, the pitched fight, in which "he would not yield even to Achilles," as Idomeneus, critically analyzing the situation, points out. As the fifteenth book draws to its sonorous, orchestral close, bringing Hector to the ships and the Achaeans to the brink of destruction, Ajax calls out three times to his troops, each time with the brief and grim eloquence that characterizes him. The first of these outcries begins with a call to *aidôs,* and the second is wholly given to it. It is impossible to translate with anything like the poetic force of the original this moving appeal to the soldiers not to break and flee, but to "reverence each other," and fight for each other's sake. Less pointed, but still insistent on the need for mutual and self-reliance is the great last speech:

> O friends, heroes, Danaoi, comrades of Ares,
> Be men, fellows, remember your rushing valor.
> What? can we say we have any helpers behind us,
> Any warlike bulwark, to ward destruction from men?
> No, no city is near us fitted with towers
> Where with an allied people we might be saved.
> Here in the plain of the close-mailed Trojans we lie,
> Toppling against the sea, far from the land of our fathers;
> So in our hands is light, not in a yielding from war.
>
> (bk. 15, ll. 733–41)

Words, one feels, are squeezed out of Ajax only with difficulty, and these rise from grim depths indeed. It is his massive and steadfast devotion, not brilliant display, which makes Ajax what he is, both here in the Great

Battle, and elsewhere. For all his clear personality, the *Iliad* represents him primarily as a hero among heroes, a fighter shoulder to shoulder with friends, mighty yet modest.

As such, the contrast with Achilles is, of course, sharp. In the Embassy Ajax makes only one brief speech, but it is fully in character. While Odysseus proceeds with diplomatic tact and design, and Achilles himself and Phoenix probe the deeper meanings of the situation, Ajax stresses the simple social level. He rebukes Achilles for his lack of human regard for his fellows, and calls upon him to remember *aidôs*:

> But Achilles
> Has a wild, great-hearted spirit in his breast,
> Wretch, and cares not for the love of his friends,
> Wherewith we honor him above all by the ships,
> Cruel . . .
>
> . . . .
>   Do you put on a gentle spirit,
> Reverence your roof; under your roof, take heed, we are,
> From the host of the Greeks, desire to be to you
> Closest and dearest of all the Achaeans.
>
>   (bk. 9, ll. 628–42)

By no means unmoved by the claims of humanity, Achilles grants Ajax his point, but holds to his wrath. But the view which Ajax expresses has been deliberately reserved for him by the poet, and it is carried out subsequently in the way Ajax bears the chief brunt of Achilles' defection. Odysseus, Diomedes, and Agamemnon come off with slight wounds. Ajax suffers it out to the end, and, as if to emphasize the contrast between the visionary exaltation of Achilles and Ajax's desperate immersion in immediate realities, Homer slips a brief glimpse of the battlefield between the long speech of Achilles in 16 and the arming of Patroclus. The speech ends with a weird and terrible wish for himself and Patroclus:

> Would, O Father Zeus and Athena and Apollo
> Not one man of the Trojans might flee death, many as they are,
> Not one man of the Argives, but we two, putting off death,
> Alone might break the holy crown of Troy.

> Thus they spoke such things to each other.
> But Ajax no longer was holding out; he was driven by missiles;
> Zeus' plan and the glorious Trojans were conquering him,
> Smiting and smiting; and round his temples his shining helmet

Stricken rang terribly, and always the blows fell
On his well-wrought visor; and his left shoulder sagged
Holding still the painted shield firm; yet round him
Crowding with missiles, they could not stagger him.
Always his breath came hard, the sweat poured down
Heavily from all his limbs, nor could he rest;
Everywhere evil was piled on evil.

(bk. 16, ll. 97–111)

If the poet chose to paint so vividly the plight of Ajax in this particular place, in the middle of a scene otherwise devoted to Achilles and Patroclus, it could only be because he wished to show that the wrath of Achilles, and the plan of Zeus, while bad for everybody, put the most suffering of all on the most loyal and innocent man in the host. The position of Ajax begins to take on almost tragic shape, foreshadowing the tragic function of Patroclus. A few lines later, the head of his spear is hacked off, and Ajax recognizes, with horror, the hand of Zeus in the Trojan victory. He retreats at last, and fire falls on the ships. Throughout the poem, Ajax is unique in having no direct dealing with any god; the nearest approaches to such are, besides this passage, a few places where Zeus sends him an omen, or blows away the mist, when Ajax prays him to slay the Achaeans in the light. When the other Achaeans are wounded, Ajax is not; instead he is cast into a momentary irrational fear by Zeus, and retreats confusedly. It is always Zeus on these occasions, the Zeus who is favoring Achilles, a fact which further emphasizes Ajax's relation to the Wrath. But in general it is not his stance in regard to the absolute world of the gods which reveals the nature of Ajax; it is his relations with the other human characters, his fellow warriors.

In the early part of the *Iliad,* he appears little, and then more as part of the panorama than as a character. His description is surprisingly brief in the Teichoscopia, or View from the Wall, and his duel with Hector is not specially impressive. Yet even in these two passages, confined as they are to mere externals, one gets a glimpse of the man, huge, broad-shouldered, of brief speech, and "smiling with his terrible eyebrows" as he stalks up to the lists. When this sketch is filled out in the rest of the poem, the figure of Ajax reveals itself, like that of Agamemnon, as an especial masterpiece of the transformation of traditional material into character.

Some Homeric characterizations are limited portraits, acutely drawn but confined to one or two scenes: for example, Paris and Helen, who scarcely appear except in books 3 and 6; Pandarus, in early 4 and early 5; Andromache, only in 6, 22, and 24, the elegiac books; Teucer, who is fully visible only in 8 and in three or four passages of the Great Battle. Others, such as Glaucus, Sarpedon, and Aeneas, have numerous recurrent appearances, but, consistent as they may be, their characters play no great role in the continuity of the poem. The characters analyzed above, together, of course, with Achilles and Hector, who will be treated elsewhere, have a great deal to do with the poem's continuity. Each represents a purposeful crystallization of a general heroic figure, specifically developed along lines appropriate to the *Iliad,* and no better proof exists of the unity of the poem than the unity of conception underlying not merely the primary figures, but even these secondary ones, subordinated as they are to the major action and the transcendent concept of heroism in Achilles. Ajax and Diomedes, both normative in a way, the one of heroic endurance and *aidôs,* the other of brilliant daring and glory; Nestor, the embodiment of the rules of the heroic game; Agamemnon, the king deluded by the pretensions of power, yet essentially helpless; Ajax son of Oileus, the violent ruffian; even Thersites, the truthful boor; these are all, after one fashion or another, brought into revealing contrast with Achilles, and through this contrast Homer has succeeded in unifying the panoramic aspect of the epic with the dramatic structure which he has imposed. There can be no question of large chunks of epic material thrust raw into an *Achilleis*; everything has been reconceived with minutest care. Given the same plot and episode, the Roman Lucan might well have made Ajax his principal figure; Virgil, one suspects, could have performed some very different wonders with Agamemnon. Homer fashioned Achilles, and refashioned all the other characters in the story to fit him.

One other character belongs to this group: Odysseus. In his case, we have the *Odyssey* to aid in understanding the latitude enjoyed by the composers of epic in the treatment of a traditional motif or character. For the moment it is irrelevant whether the *Odyssey* be by the same hand as the *Iliad* or not, because the common denominator of both views of Odysseus is easily discernible, and may be reasonably taken as the traditional core of the character. Resourcefulness and trickery form the essence of it, both implying survival by adjustment, either self-adjustment or a skillful manipulation of circumstances. Part of the fascination of Greek character, today as in antiquity, is the interplay of this quality with its opposite, heroic inflexibility. Each implies a distinct view of what reality is: Odysseus sees reality as the situation or problem before him; Achilles sees it as something in himself, and the problem is to identify himself with it completely, through action. In both *Iliad* and *Odyssey,* Odysseus is fully the man of survival by adjustment. In the *Odyssey,* however, his ability to survive is viewed not merely as resourcefulness, but also as a kind of tough, moral stamina in the resistance to adversity, the quality called *tlemosyne* in Greek, and repeatedly emphasized in the epithet "much-enduring." Moreover, his "many devices" now take on a more genuinely intellectual coloring, so that in the *Odyssey,* Odysseus is developed into the first Occidental prototype of the *uomo universale,* the man who has seen everything, can do everything, and understands everything. Reality is that which he finds before him, but there is nothing trivial in what a penetrating man finds before him; Odysseus finds in his wanderings the vast archetypal patterns of things which are—brute force in Cyclops, and its opposite in the finely civilized Phaeacians; kind hosts (like Aeolus) who feed and help you, and Laestrygonians who eat you; temptations to oblivion in the Lotus-eaters and those counterfeit Muses, the Sirens; sex in its dangerous and deathlike aspect in Circe, and in all its youthful delicacy in Nausicaa; death itself in the quest of Teiresias's knowledge of the unknowable. In such an expansion of the theme, Homer has turned his resourceful man into Man the Resourceful Indomitable Seeker of all things which are, anticipating Sophocles' famous ode in the *Antigone.* The theme of trickery runs throughout, but subordinated to this main idea, dominating chiefly in the later books, where the suitors are slain by trick.

The Odysseus of the *Iliad* is quite the same man in essence, but viewed differently. Resourcefulness and trick are still the cornerstones of his nature, but a different structure rises on them. The cleverest in the army, he is the right-hand man of Agamemnon, and "shares his thoughts with him." As the deviser of the wooden horse, and the captor, with Diomedes, of the Palladium of Troy, he was, according to tradition, one of the most useful, if not the most useful, of all the Achaeans to the cause. Both his basic characteristics contribute to this usefulness. In the second book, when the army rushes for the ships, it is the quick thinking of Odysseus, inspired as always by Athena, who restrains the men, and saves the face of Agamemnon. Immediately after this episode, he makes his first appearance as orator and chief diplomat of the host, in the long speech about the hopeful portent at Aulis. In this capacity he appears again in Antenor's reminiscences of him, and in the Embassy to Achilles. As the embodiment of craft, and the complementary antitype of Achilles, as well as of Ajax, he represents in the context of the *Iliad* one of the chief forces which took Troy. Achilles and Ajax are lonely figures, and combine with nobody; but the more flexible man of war, Diomedes, combines very well with Odysseus to form a deadly team in book 10 (if genuine), where the theft of Rhesus's horses, like so many episodes in the *Iliad,* is possibly a transference of the theft of the Palladium into terms appropriate to this particular stage of the action.

Guileful, and always ready with an adjustment, Odysseus never in the *Iliad* exposes himself to unnecessary danger. His contrast with Diomedes in this respect is subtly accented in book 8, when Diomedes, seeing Nestor in peril of his life and unable to flee with the others before the advancing Trojans, calls to Odysseus to help rescue him from the tangled reins of his horses. Odysseus prudently keeps running, and Diomedes alone comes to Nestor's aid. Homer wastes no words condemning Odysseus's will to live on this occasion; rather the opposite, for a few lines later he makes Nestor himself say to Diomedes,

> Son of Tydeus, turn again to flight your horses of cleftless hoof!
> Do you not know that victory follows you not from Zeus?
> Now Zeus son of Kronos ordains the glory to this man,
> Today; but another time, if he wills, to us he will also
> Grant it.
>
> (bk. 8, ll. 139–43)

Evidently the rule book included the specifications for living to fight another day, without prejudice to one's heroic claims. Common sense was not to be excluded, and Odysseus in the *Iliad* has a large share of it. And this common sense, which by no means marks Odysseus in the *Odyssey* (his companions are always reproving him for lack of it), is nevertheless the product of the same will to live which motivates so much of the *Odyssey*. The tradition of resourcefulness and adjustment has taken its own direction in the *Iliad*. In the battle scenes, especially where he is wounded, his cool wary outlook comes clear; he wins by a trick where he cannot by force, and saves himself by keeping his head and getting next to Ajax.

Yet, if his common-sense view of reality can sometimes look like cowardice, it has also its human and penetrating side. Agamemnon, always ready to retreat, proposes launching the ships to keep the Trojans from burning them; once launched, they might as well be used to go home, under cover of night. Odysseus's reply is finely sarcastic. Not only is Agamemnon's suggestion low spirited and unworthy of an Achaean king; it is also utterly unrealistic to think that the ships could be launched and the Trojans held off at the same time; even to try it would spell destruction. And he concludes his speech by addressing the king with a formula which strikes the ear with extreme irony, under the circumstances: "O marshaler of hosts." Humbled, Agamemnon asks for advice, and gets a more spirited proposal from Diomedes.

But, as in so many other cases, the character of Odysseus in the *Iliad* reveals itself most clearly in the scenes with Achilles. The chief polarities of the Embassy lie in the speeches of Phoenix and Achilles, so that here the latter's contrast with Odysseus is at most lightly sketched, in the juxtaposition of Odysseus's skilled, effective appeal and the chaotic eloquence of Achilles' reply. Odysseus begins with a graceful compliment for Achilles' hospitality; he outlines the danger of the Greek army, then weighs Achilles' incurable remorse in after time, if he does not rescue the host, with the honor he will receive if he does; he repeats the long list of Agamemnon's peace offerings; and the speech ends with another compliment, a flattering appeal to Achilles' supreme valor. It is perfectly constructed oratory, with exordium, exposition, arguments, and peroration. Cool, supple, and contrived, it moves Achilles not at all, as do the speeches of Phoenix and Ajax, and compared with it, the hero's answer is like a storm at sea, as he ignores all the arguments, and heaps scorn on Agamemnon's gifts.

The real conflict between Odysseus and Achilles comes in book 19, the scene of the renunciation of the Wrath. Agamemnon, admitting his fault, wants to give the amends he had promised, but Achilles puts him off; he longs for the war without delay, and Agamemnon may give his gifts some other time, or keep them. Odysseus intervenes with the argument that it is going to be a long fight, and that the army will perform better on a full stomach; first let the men eat and Agamemnon give his gifts and entertain Achilles. Achilles again refuses; he will touch nothing until he has avenged Patroclus, whereupon Odysseus puts the claims of common sense more movingly:

> O Achilles, Peleus' son, far the best of Achaeans,
> Greater you are than I, and better by not a little
> With spears; but I in thinking, I surpass you
> Much, for I am older and know more.
> So, let your heart endure my words.
> Swiftly on men comes a sick surfeit of battle-din
> Where bronze strews the ground with much straw
> And the harvest is least, when Zeus tilts the balances,
> He who is steward of the war of men.
> Not by a fast can the Achaeans mourn their dead;
> Too many and frequent every day they fall.
> When shall any get breathing-time from the toil?
> Him who dies we must bury, having hearts
> Firm, and weeping for him but on that day.
> Those who are left amid the hateful war,
> They must remember drink and food, that rather still

> Ceaselessly we may fight with our enemies,
> Clothing our bodies in weariless bronze.
>
> (bk. 19, ll. 216–33)

Achilles does not answer this, and though he allows the delay for food and gifts, he eats nothing himself, and is instead sustained by a divine distillate of nectar and ambrosia, brought by Athena. The presence of Odysseus in this scene makes clear, as few other things could have done, that Achilles, in renouncing his wrath, has not returned to the same world from which he retired. The council, in which he quarreled with Agamemnon in the first place, had been called by Achilles, out of concern for the army's welfare: he had then been integrally united with the others. Nothing is farther from his thoughts now; Odysseus must remind him of the limits of time and humanity. Nor is there any real reconcilement with Agamemnon; the gracious formalities are a bore. Only the battle counts. Yet the importance of food, even to those who mourn their dearest losses, is a motif which will arise again, when Achilles himself gently presses entertainment upon Priam. But again, Homer miraculously transforms the motif. What is simple sense to Odysseus becomes in Achilles a token of mysterious, infinite compassion:

> Hark you, your son is ransomed, old man, as you bade;
> He lies on a bier; you yourself, with the glimpse of dawn
> Shall see as you take him away; now, let us remember food.
> Even fair-haired Niobe remembered food,
> She whose twelve children perished in her halls,
> Six daughters, and six flourishing sons.
>
> . . . .
>
> Yet she remembered food, when she was weary of weeping.
> Now somewhere among cliffs, in the sheep-pastured
>   mountains,
> Sipylus, where they tell of the couches of heavenly
> Nymphs, who dance around the Achelous,
> There, stone that she is, she broods on the gods' afflictions.
> Come then, let us also, divine old man, consider
> Food.
>
> (bk. 24, ll. 599–619)

There is a wonderful passage in the *Odyssey* where Odysseus meets the ghost of Achilles in Hades. They are profoundly courteous to each other. Odysseus, outlining his own toils, reminds Achilles that the supreme honor which the latter receives from all makes light of death; but Achilles, complimenting Odysseus on the magnificence of his adventures, answers that there is no consolation in death, for it is better to be the living slave of a poor man than king of the all the dead. Yet, it is hard to imagine Achilles as the slave of a poor man, and hard to believe that he is speaking a literal truth. He is emphasizing the cost of his greatness, the incurable sorrow of being Achilles. He is saying, I have suffered the worst, and identified myself with it; you have merely survived. And Odysseus, for his part, says: you are very honored indeed, but you are dead; I am doing the really difficult and great thing. In the retrospective air of Hades, Homer can thus summarize the gulf between the two men, and their characteristic views of life, in a few lines. But the same gulf appears in the *Iliad,* subtly limned in books 9 and 19.

We do not know anything substantial about pre-Homeric poetry, but the consistently warlike and generalized nature of the formulaic epithets, as well as of the stock-in-trade motifs of battle, council, secret exploit, discouragement, assistance by gods, sacrifice, and all the rest, which are Homer's material, indicate a vast array of malleable rudiments, out of which the singer made what he could. With singleness of vision and real mastery of the rudiments, a poet might so dispose and deploy his material that the generalized motifs, crystallized phrases, and traditional imagery fall into contextual groupings of great specific significance. This seems to be what Homer has done. At every point the tradition supplied him with an abundance of what might be said. We cannot always follow his selective process, or know what he omitted altogether; but what he chose to say was so timed in context, combination, and contrast that his characters, from the most primary ones to those fleeting personalities who appear only as they fall on the battlefield, possess a haunting kind of individuality, an individuality which forces its way, by the poet's skill, through the universal heroic type. Something, undoubtedly, was due to predecessors; but the consistent unity of these characters is Homer's own.

Homer's View of Man

Bruno Snell

We find it difficult to conceive of a mentality which made no provision for
the body as such. Among the early expressions designating what was later
rendered as *sōma* or "body," only the plurals *guia, melea* (both "limbs"),
etc., refer to the physical nature of the body; for *chrōs* is merely the limit of
the body, and *demas* represents the frame, the structure, and occurs only in
the accusative of specification. As it is, early Greek art actually corroborates
our impression that the physical body of man was comprehended, not as a
unit but as an aggregate. Not until the classical art of the fifth century do we
find attempts to depict the body as an organic unit whose parts are mutually
correlated. In the preceding period the body is a mere construct of independent parts variously put together. It must not be thought, however, that the
pictures of human beings from the time of Homer are like the primitive
drawings to which our children have accustomed us, though they too simply add limb to limb. Our children usually represent the human shape as
shown in figure 1, whereas figure 2 reproduces the Greek concept as found
on the vases of the geometric period.

Our children first draw a body as the central and most important part
of their design; then they add the head, the arms and the legs. The geometric figures, on the other hand, lack this central part; they are nothing but
melea kai guia, i.e., limbs with strong muscles, separated from each other by
means of exaggerated joints. This difference is of course partially dependent
upon the clothes they wore, but even after we have made due allowance for

From *The Discovery of the Mind: The Greek Origins of European Thought,* translated by
T. G. Rosenmeyer. © 1953 by Basil Blackwell Publishers.

49

this the fact remains that the Greeks of this early period seem to have seen in a strangely "articulated" way. In their eyes the individual limbs are clearly distinguished from each other, and the joints are, for the sake of emphasis, presented as extraordinarily thin, while the fleshy parts are made to bulge just as unrealistically. The early Greek drawing seeks to demonstrate the agility of the human figure, the drawing of the modern child its compactness and unity.

Thus the early Greeks did not, either in their language or in the visual arts, grasp the body as a unit. The phenomenon is the same as with the verbs denoting sight; in the latter, the activity is at first understood in terms of its conspicuous modes, of the various attitudes and sentiments connected with it, and it is a long time before speech begins to address itself to the essential function of this activity. It seems, then, as if language aims progressively to express the essence of an act, but is at first unable to comprehend it because it is a function, and as such neither tangibly apparent nor associated with certain unambiguous emotions. As soon, however, as it is recognized and has received a name, it has come into existence, and the knowledge of its existence quickly becomes common property. Concerning the body, the chain of events may have been somewhat like this: in the early period a speaker, when faced by another person, was apparently satisfied to call out his name: this is Achilles, or to say: this is a man. As a next step, the most conspicuous elements of his appearance are described, namely his limbs as existing side by side; their functional correlation is not apprehended in its full importance until somewhat later. True enough, the function is a concrete fact, but its objective existence does not manifest itself so clearly as the presence of the individual corporeal limbs, and its prior significance escapes even the owner of the limbs himself. With the discovery of this hidden unity, of course, it is at once appreciated as an immediate and self-explanatory truth.

This objective truth, it must be admitted, does not exist for man until it is seen and known and designated by a word; until, thereby, it has become an object of thought. Of course the Homeric man had a body exactly like the later Greeks, but he did not know it qua body, but merely as the sum total of his limbs. This is another way of saying that the Homeric Greeks did not yet have a body in the modern sense of the word; body, *sōma*, is a later interpretation of what was originally comprehended as *melē* or *guia*, i.e., as limbs. Again and again Homer speaks of fleet legs, of knees in speedy motion, of sinewy arms; it is in these limbs, immediately evident as they are to his eyes, that he locates the secret of life.

To return now to the intellect and the soul, we find there too the same perspective. Again Homer has no one word to characterize the mind or the soul. *Psyche,* the word for soul in later Greek, has no original connexion with the thinking and feeling soul. For Homer, *psyche* is the force which keeps the human being alive. There is, therefore, a gap in the Homeric vocabulary, comparable to the deficiency in "physical" terminology which we discussed above. As before, the gap is filled with a number of words which do not possess the same centre of gravity as the modern terms, but which cover more or less the same area. For the area of the "soul," the most important words are *psyche, thymos,* and *noos.* Concerning the *psyche* Homer says that it forsakes man at the moment of death, and that it flutters about in Hades; but it is impossible to find out from his words what he considers to be the function of the *psyche* during man's lifetime. There is no lack of theories about the nature of the *psyche* prior to death, but so far from relying on the testimony of the Homeric poems they are based only on conjectures and analogies. One would do well to remember how little Homer says about the *psyche* of the living and of the dying man; for one thing, it leaves its owner when he is dying, or when he loses consciousness; secondly he says that the *psyche* is risked in battle, a battle is fought for it, one wishes to save his *psyche,* and so forth. There is no justification here for assuming two different connotations of *psyche,* for although we shall have occasion to translate it as "life," that is not its true meaning. The *psyche* which is the prize of battle, which is risked, and saved, is identical with the soul which departs from a dying man.

Of this departure, Homer mentions only a few details. The *psyche* leaves through the mouth, it is breathed forth; or again it leaves through a wound, and then flies off to Hades. There it leads a ghostlike existence, as the spectre (*eidōlon*) of the deceased. The word *psyche* is akin to *psychein,* "to breathe," and denotes the breath of life which of course departs through the mouth; the escape from a wound evidently represents a secondary development. This vital breath is, as it were, a semiconcrete organ which exists in a man as long as he lives. As for its location, and its function, Homer passes them over in silence, and that means that we cannot know about them either. It appears as if in Homeric times the term *psyche* chiefly evoked the notion of an eschatological soul; at one point Homer says: he has but one *psyche,* he is mortal (bk. 21, l. 569); when, however, he wants to say "as long as the breath of life remains in a man" he avoids the word and puts it (bk. 10, l. 89), "as long as my breath remains in my breast and my knees are in motion." Yet in spite of the mention of breath or respiration, the presence of the verb "remain" suggests that the notion of the *psyche* is also involved, and that therefore Homer has a concept of the "breath of life."

The other two words for the "mind" are *thymos* and *noos. Thymos* in Homer is the generator of motion or agitation, while *noos* is the cause of ideas and images. All mental phenomena are in one way or another distributed so as to fall in the sphere of either of the two organs. In several passages death is depicted as a departure of the *thymos,* with the result that scholars have attempted to interpret *thymos* as "soul," rivalling the *psyche.* "The *thymos* left his bones" is a phrase which occurs seven times; "quickly the *thymos* went forth from the limbs" is found twice. If we translate *thymos* as "organ of (e)motion," the matter becomes simple enough. Since this organ, prominently among its functions, determines physical motion, it is plausible enough to say that at the point of death the *thymos* leaves the bones and the *melē,* i.e., the limbs with their muscles. But this hardly implies that the *thymos* continues to exist after death; it merely means: what provided motion for the bones and the limbs is now gone.

Other passages in which *thymos* and *psyche* are apparently used without any distinction in meaning are more difficult to explain. [In] book 22, line 67, Homer says, "when someone by stroke or throw of the sharp bronze has bereft my *rhethē* of *thymos.*" At this point the meaning of *rhethē* must be "limbs"; the concept is the same as in the verse just quoted, viz., that the *thymos* departs from the limbs, and this explanation was already given by the ancients. The difficulty arises when we come to the other passages which contain *rhethē;* book 16, line 856 and book 22, line 363: "his *psyche* fled from his *rhethē* and went down to Hades." This is unique, for ordinarily the *psyche* leaves the body through the mouth (bk. 9, l. 409) or through a wound (bk. 14, l. 518; bk. 16, l. 505), i.e., through an aperture of the body. The expression "from the limbs," besides being considerably less plausible and convincing, also presupposes that the soul has its seat in the limbs, a view which is not met with elsewhere in Homer. Now it so happens that the word *rhethos* remained alive in Aeolic, but not in the sense of "limb"; we take this information from the scholia on the verse cited above, whence we conclude that for Sappho and Alcaeus *rhethos* bore the meaning "face." From the Aeolic poets this meaning of the word was handed on to Sophocles (*Antigone* 529), Euripides (*Heracles* 1204) and Theocritus (29.16). As the same scholion tells us, Dionysius Thrax already came to the conclusion that in Homer too *rhethos* must refer to the face. Other ancient scholars opposed him by pointing to the circumstance that in Homer the *psyche* sometimes leaves the body through a wound. In any case, the solution offered by Dionysius is too simple, for as has already been stated, in book 22, line 68 we read that the *thymos* takes its leave from the *rhethē* and they must be the *melē,* for if our interpretation of *thymos* as (e)motion is right, it may be expected to escape from the limbs but not from the face, let alone the mouth. Book 16, line 856, on the other hand, concerns the *psyche,* and here we are not surprised that it should fly off through the mouth.

The whole confusion is easily resolved once we take into consideration the age of the various passages. Book 22, line 68 is undoubtedly very late, probably even, as E. Kapp has pointed out to me, dependent on Tyrtaeus. The author is someone who was not conversant with the Aeolic word *rhethos,* and whose understanding of Homer's language was on the whole no longer perfect. Confronted with such seemingly analogous passages as book 13, line 671, "the *thymos* quickly went from his limbs (*melē*)," and book 16, line 856, "his *psyche* escaped from the *rhethē* and went down to Hades," he was quick to equate *psyche* with *thymos* and *melē* with *rhethē,* and by a further analogy with a passage like book 5, line 317 he finally formed his own verse. By the standard of Homer's own usage, these words make no sense at all. There are other indications that the concepts of *thymos* and *psyche* are easily confused: book 7, line 131 reads, "his *thymos* escaped from his limbs (*melē*) down to Hades." It has long been noticed that the idea of the *thymos* going down to Hades contradicts the usual Homeric conception. The verse is contaminated from book 13, ll. 671f., "quickly the *thymos* went forth from the limbs (*melē*)," and book 3, line 322, "grant that he dies and goes down to Hades." It is just possible that the contamination is the work of a later poet who did not know the Homeric usage. But it is more likely that it was brought about by a rhapsode who confused several sections of verses in his memory, a common enough occurrence in oral delivery. In that case emendation would seem to be called for, and as it happens another part of a verse from Homer furnishes an easy remedy. In book 16, line 856 (and bk. 22, l. 362) we have a reading which is good and meaningful: "the soul [*psyche*] flew down to Hades from the *rhethē*." From this, book 7, line 131 may be reconstructed: [the *psyche* escaped from the *rhethē* down to Hades]. It is true that there remain a number of passages in which *thymos* is the eschatological soul which flies off at the moment of death; but in each case it is the death of an animal which is so described—the death of a horse (bk. 16, l. 469), of a stag (*Odyssey,* bk. 10, l. 163), of a boar (*Odyssey,* bk. 19, l. 454), or of a dove (bk. 23, l. 880). I have no doubt that the origin of this usage was as follows: evidently people were averse to ascribing the *psyche,* which a human being loses when he dies, also to an animal. They therefore invented the idea of a *thymos* which leaves the animal when it expires. The idea was suggested by the passages which exhibit the *thymos* leaving the limbs or the bones of a man. Those passages in turn which speak of a *thymos* of animals contributed their share to the confusion between *thymos* and *psyche.* But the phrase "the *thymos* flew off" which occurs four times, i.e., with comparative frequency, is always applied to animals—and, incidentally, to no one more than once. This proves that in the early period the two terms were not yet used interchangeably.

Whereas the contrast between *thymos* and *psyche* is clear and emphatic, the line between *thymos* and *noos* cannot be drawn with the same precision. If, as we have suggested, *thymos* is the mental organ which causes (e)motion, while *noos* is the recipient of images, the *noos* may be said generally to be in charge of intellectual matters, and *thymos* of things emotional. Yet they overlap in many respects. Today, for instance, we regard the head as the seat of thinking, and the heart as the organ of feeling; but that does not prevent us from saying: he carries thoughts of his beloved in his heart— where the heart becomes the seat of thinking, but the thoughts are oriented towards love; or the reverse: he has nothing in his head but revenge—and here again the meaning is: thoughts of vengeance. But these exceptions are only apparent, for they are easily replaced by equivalent turns of expression: he has vengeance in his heart, etc. The same is true of *thymos* = (e)motion and *noos* = understanding; the exceptions which might be cited by way of argument against these equations are not real. Nevertheless it is only fair to concede that the distinction between *thymos* and *noos* is not as evident as that between *thymos* and *psyche.* Here are a few examples.

Ordinarily the sensation of joy is located in the *thymos.* But [in] *Odyssey,* book 8, line 78 we read: Agamemnon rejoiced in his *noos* when Achilles and Odysseus quarreled with each other for the distinction of being the best man. Agamemnon's delight does not spring from the altercation of the two most valiant heroes—that would be absurd—but from his recollection of Apollo's prophecy that Troy would fall when the best heroes contended with one another. The basis of his joy, therefore, is reflection.

Another instance: generally speaking it is the *thymos* which rouses a man to action. But [in] book 14, lines 61f. Nestor says, "Let us take counsel . . . if the *noos* may accomplish anything." In this passage *thymos* would be quite meaningless, for Nestor asks them to consider whether "counsel," i.e., an idea, may achieve anything. Although the *thymos* is customarily the abode of joy, pleasure, love, sympathy, anger, and all mental agitation, occasionally we also find knowledge residing in it. [In] book 2, line 409, for example, we are told that Menelaus did not have to be summoned to the assembly, for "he knew in his *thymos* that his brother was beset by trouble." He knew it, not because he had been informed, or because his perception was especially acute, but by virtue of his instincts, through brotherly sympathy. Or, in the words of the poet, he knew it through an "emotion." Examples of this sort could be multiplied freely. *Noos* is akin to *noein* which means "to realize," "to see in its true colours"; and often it may simply be translated as "to see." Witness book 5, line 590: "She saw (*enoēse*) Hector in the ranks." Frequently it is combined with *idein,* but it stands for a type of seeing which involves not merely visual activity but the mental act which goes with the vision. This puts it close to *gignōskein.* But the latter means "to recognize"; it is properly used of the identification of a man, while *noein* refers more particularly to situations; it means: "to acquire a clear image of something." Hence the significance of *noos.* It is the mind as a recipient of clear images, or, more briefly, the organ of clear images: book 16, line 688, "The *noos* of Zeus is ever stronger than that of men." *Noos* is, as it were, the mental eye which exercises an unclouded vision. But given a slight shift which in Greek is easily managed, *noos* may come to denote the function rather than the organ. In its capacity as a permanent function *noos* represents the faculty of having clear ideas, i.e., the power of intelligence: book 13, line 730, "To one man the god has given works of war . . . but in the heart of another far-seeing Zeus has placed an excellent *noos.*" At this point the meaning "mind" shades off into the notion of "thinking." The two are of course closely related; in our language we employ the term "intelligence" to refer both to the intellect and to its activity or capacity. From here it is only a short step, and *noos* will signify also the individual act, the individual image, or the thought. We read, for instance, that someone thinks a *noos*: book 9, line 104 and *Odyssey,* book 5, line 23. Thus the area covered by this term exceeds the competence of our words mind, soul, or intelligence. The same is also true of *thymos.* If it is said that someone feels something in his *thymos,* the reference is to an organ which we may translate as "soul" provided we keep in mind that it is the soul as the seat of (e)motions. But *thymos* may also serve as the name of a function, in which case we render it as "will" or "character"; and where it refers to one single act, the word once more transcends the limitations of our "soul" or "mind." The most obvious example occurs in the *Odyssey*, book 9, line 302, where Odysseus says, "Another *thymos* held me back"; each individual impulse, therefore, is also a *thymos*.

What bearing does all this have on our investigation of Homer's attitude towards the human mind? At first it might be suspected that *thymos* and *noos* are nothing more than the parts of the soul, such as we know from Plato's psychology. But those parts presuppose a psychic whole of which Homer has no cognizance. *Thymos, noos,* and *psyche* as well are separate organs, each having its own particular function. We say "to look at a thing with different eyes," without meaning to refer to the organ; the idea that someone provides himself with another set of eyes would hardly arise. Rather, the word "eye" here stands for "function of the eye," "vision," and what we actually mean is "to see with a different view." Homer's "another *thymos*" must be similarly understood. But that is not all: the two passages with *noos* cited above (bk. 9, l. 104 and *Odyssey*, bk. 5, l. 23) lead us even further, in a most significant direction. *Noos* as understood in their context no longer refers to the function itself but to the result of the *noein*. *Noon ameinona noēsei* still lends itself to the translation: "he will devise a better thought." But now thought has ceased to be the activity of thinking, and has become the thing thought. *Touton ebouleusas noon* [you counselled this thought] presents the same situation. It is worth pointing out, however, that *noos,* in the only two Homeric passages where it is to be rendered as "thought," appears as the internal object of *noein* and *bouleuein* [counsel, advise]. The *actio verbi* of *noein,* i.e., the function, obviously remains a decisive factor.

We have intentionally avoided bringing into our inquiry the distinction, on the face of it so pertinent, between "concrete" and "abstract." Actually this distinction is for our purposes open to question, and not nearly so fruitful as the difference between organ and function. It might, for instance, be thought that because the word *athymos* [without *thymos*] is found in one Homeric passage, *thymos* must already have possessed an abstract significance. But if that were so, one would have to admit that "heart" and "head" are abstracts too, for it is entirely feasible to say that someone is heartless, or has lost his head. If I declare that someone has a good brain, and I mean his thinking; or: someone has a soft heart, and I mean his feelings, I use the name of the organ in place of that of the function. "Heartless," "brainless," and *athymos* refer to the lack of a function. The metaphoric use of words for organs, which may be interpreted as abstraction, has its place on the most primitive level of speech, for it is precisely on that level that the organ is regarded, not as dead and concrete, but as participating in its function.

As soon as we attempt to describe the mental concepts of Homer by means of the catchwords "organ" and "function" we are bound to encounter terminological difficulties such as always arise for anyone who wishes to reproduce foreign idioms and peculiarities within the terms of his own tongue. If I say that the *thymos* is a mental organ, that it is the organ of a psychic process, I find myself caught in phrases which contain a contradiction in terms, for in our eyes the ideas of the soul and of an organ are incompatible. To express myself accurately I should have to say: what we interpret as the soul, Homeric man splits up into three components each of which he defines by the analogy of physical organs. Our transcription of *psyche, noos,* and *thymos* as "organs" of life, of perception, and of (e)motion are, therefore, merely in the nature of abbreviations, neither totally accurate nor exhaustive; this could not be otherwise, owing to the circumstance that the concept of the "soul"—and also of the "body," as we have seen—is tied up with the whole character and orientation of a language. This means that in the various languages we are sure to find the most divergent interpretations of these ideas.

According to some the remark that Homer had "not yet" acquired the knowledge of many things lowers his stature. Consequently they have tried to explain the difference between his mentality and ours by the proposition that Homer stylized his thinking, that for aesthetic or other reasons he avoided the description of mental processes because such details might have detracted from the grand simplicity of his heroes. Is it conceivable that Homer could deliberately have turned his back upon the notions of "intellect" and "soul"? Such psychological finesse, affecting the most subtle particulars, cannot in all fairness be attributed to the ancient epic poet. What is more, the gaps left by Homer's "ignorance" suddenly fall into a meaningful pattern if they are set off against those of his notions which our modern thinking seems to lack. Deliberate stylization is undoubtedly to be found in Homer, but this is not one of the quarters in which it takes effect. Do we expect Homer to present us with that invention of Goethe's humour, Little Mr. Microcosm? Everything human, and especially everything great, is one-sided and confined within limits. The belief in the existence of a universal, uniform human mind is a rationalist prejudice.

Actually there is further evidence for our contention that we are dealing with an early stage of European thought, and not with stylization. That Homer's conception of *thymos, noos,* and *psyche* still depended to a large extent on an analogy with the physical organs becomes a matter of absolute certainty if we turn to that era of transition when his conception began to be abandoned. To be sure, the evidence for the use of the words *sōma* and *psyche* during the period extending from Homer to the fifth century is not full enough to allow us to trace the origin of the new meanings "body" and "soul" in every detail. Apparently they were evolved as complementary terms, and more likely than not it was *psyche* which first started on its course, perhaps under the influence of notions concerning the immortality of the soul. The word denoting the eschatological soul was put to a new use, to designate the soul as a whole, and the word for corpse came to be employed for the living body; the reason for this must be that the element which provided man during his living days with emotions, perceptions, and thoughts was believed to survive in the *psyche*. Presumably people felt that animate man had within him a spiritual or intellectual portion, though they were unable to define this element by one term sufficiently accurate and inclusive. As a matter of fact, this is the state of affairs which we shall meet among the early writers of lyric poetry. And it may be inferred that, because the eschatological *psyche* had been correlated with the *sōma* of the dead, the new *psyche,* the "soul," demanding a body to suit it, caused the term *sōma* to be extended so that it was ultimately used also of the living body. But whatever the details of this evolution, the distinction between body and soul represents a "discovery" which so impressed people's minds that it was thereafter accepted as self-evident, in spite of the fact that the relation between body and soul, and the nature of the soul itself, continued to be the topic of lively speculation.

The first writer to feature the new concept of the soul is Heraclitus. He calls the soul of living man *psyche*; in his view man consists of body and soul, and the soul is endowed with qualities which differ radically from those of the body and the physical organs. We can safely say that these new qualities are irreconcilable with the categories of Homer's thought; he does not even dispose of the linguistic prerequisites to describe what Heraclitus predicates of the soul. The new expressions were fashioned in the period which separates Heraclitus from Homer, that is to say the era of the lyric. Heraclitus says (fr. 45), "You could not find the ends of the soul though you travelled every way, so deep is its *logos*." This notion of the depth or profundity of the soul is not unfamiliar to us; but it involves a dimension which is foreign to a physical organ or its function. To say someone has a deep hand, or a deep ear, is nonsensical, and when we talk of a deep voice, we mean something entirely different; the adjective there refers to vocal expression, not to the function of the voice. In Heraclitus the image of depth is designed to throw light on the outstanding trait of the soul and its realm: that it has its own dimension, that it is not extended in space. To describe this nonspatial substance we are of course obliged to fall back on a metaphor taken from space relations. But in the last analysis Heraclitus means to assert that the soul, as contrasted with things physical, reaches into infinity. Not Heraclitus but the lyric poets who preceded him were the first to voice this new idea, that intellectual and spiritual matters have "depth." Archaic poetry contains such words as "deep-pondering" and "deep-thinking"; concepts like "deep knowledge," "deep thinking," "deep pondering," as well as "deep pain" are common enough in the archaic period. In these expressions, the symbol of depth always points to the infinity of the intellectual and spiritual, which differentiates it from the physical.

Homeric speech does not yet know this aspect of the word "deep." It is more than an ordinary metaphor; it is almost as if speech were by this means trying to break through its confines, to trespass on a forbidden field of adventure. Nor does Homer show himself conversant with the specifically spiritual facet of "deep knowledge," "deep thinking," and so forth. . . . Quantity, not intensity, is Homer's standard of judgment. [In] book 24, line 639 Priam laments the fate of Hector: "I groan and brood over countless griefs." "To demand much," "to exhort much" is a frequent figure, even where the act of demanding or exhorting takes place only once. Our "much" offers a similar ambiguity. Never does Homer, in his descriptions of ideas or emotions, go beyond a purely spatial or quantitative definition; never does he attempt to sound their special, nonphysical nature. As far as he is concerned, ideas are conveyed through the *noos,* a mental organ which in turn is analogous to the eye; consequently "to know" is *eidenai* which is related to *idein,* "to see," and in fact originally means "to have seen." The eye, it appears, serves as Homer's model for the absorption of experiences. From this point of view the intensive coincides with the extensive; he who has seen much sufficiently often possesses intensive knowledge.

Nor does the *thymos* provide any scope for the development of a notion of intensity. This organ of (e)motion is, among other things, the seat of pain. In Homer's language, the *thymos* is eaten away or torn asunder by pain; the pain which hits the *thymos* is sharp, or immense, or heavy. The analogies are evident: just as a limb is struck by a pointed weapon or by a heavy stone, just as it may be corroded or torn into pieces, so also the *thymos.* As before, the concept of the spiritual is not divorced from the corporeal, and intensity, the proper dimension of the spiritual, receives no attention. Homer is not even acquainted with intensity in its original sense, as "tension." A tension within the soul has no more reality for him than a tension in the eye would, or a tension in the hand. Here too the predicates of the soul remain completely within the bounds set for physical organs. There are no divided feelings in Homer; not until Sappho are we to read of the bitter-sweet Eros. Homer is unable to say "half-willing, half-unwilling," instead he says "he was willing, but his *thymos* was not." This does not reflect a contradiction within one and the same organ, but the contention between a man and one of his organs; we should compare our saying "my hand desired to reach out, but I withdrew it." Two different things or substances engage in a quarrel with one another. As a result there is in Homer no genuine reflexion, no dialogue of the soul with itself.

Besides being "deep," the *logis* of Heraclitus is also a *koinon,* a "common" thing. It pervades everything, and everything shares it. Again, Homer has no vocabulary to express a concept of this sort; he cannot say that different beings are of the same spirit, that two men have the same mind, or one and the same soul, any more than he would allow that two men have one eye or one hand between them.

A third quality which Heraclitus assigns to the mental sphere also diverges from any predications which could be made of the physical organs; this means that it must clash with the thought and speech of Homer. Heraclitus says (fr. 115), "The soul has a *logos* which increases itself." Whatever the exact significance of this statement, we gather that Heraclitus ascribes to the *psyche* a *logos* capable of extending and adding to itself of its own accord; the soul is regarded as a sort of base from which certain developments are possible. It would be absurd to attach a similar *logos* to the eye, or the hand. For Homer the mental processes have no such capacity for self-induced expansion. Any augmentation of bodily or spiritual powers is effected from without, above all by the deity. In the sixteenth book of the *Iliad* Homer recounts how the dying Sarpedon with his last words implored his friend Glaucus to help him; but he too was wounded and could not come. So Glaucus prayed to Apollo to relieve him of his pain and restore to him the strength of his arms. Apollo heard his prayer, soothed his pain, and "cast strength in his *thymos.*" As in many other passages in which Homer refers to the intervention of a god, the event has nothing supernatural, or unnatural, about it. We are free to conjecture that Glaucus heard the dying call of Sarpedon, that it caused him to forget his pain, to collect his strength, and to resume the fighting. It is easy to say that Glaucus pulled himself together, that he recovered his self-control; but Homer says, and thinks, nothing of the sort: they are notions which we read back into the scene. We believe that a man advances from an earlier situation by an act of his own will, through his own power. If Homer, on the other hand, wants to explain the source of an increase in strength, he has no course but to say that the responsibility lies with a god.

The same is true in other cases. Whenever a man accomplishes, or pronounces, more than his previous attitude had led others to expect, Homer connects this, in so far as he tries to supply an explanation, with the interference of a god. It should be noted especially that Homer does not know genuine personal decisions; even where a hero is shown pondering two alternatives the intervention of the gods plays the key role. This divine meddling is, of course, a necessary complement of Homer's notions regarding the human mind and the soul. The *thymos* and the *noos* are so very little different from other physical organs that they cannot very well be looked upon as a genuine source of impulses; Aristotle's "first mover" is hidden from Homer's ken, as is the concept of any vital centre which controls the organic system. Mental and spiritual acts are due to the impact of external factors, and man is the open target of a great many forces which impinge on him, and penetrate his very core. That is the reason why Homer has so much to say about forces, why, in fact, he has so many words for our term "force": *menos, sthenos, biē, kikus, is, kratos, alkē, dynamis*. The meaning of each of these words is precise, concrete, and full of implications; so far from serving as abstract symbols of force, as do the later terms *dynamis* and *exousia* which may be used of no matter what function, Homer's words refer to specific functions and particular provinces of experience. *Menos* is the force in the limbs of a man who is burning to tackle a project. *Alkē* is the defensive force which helps to ward off the enemy. *Sthenos* is the muscular force of the body, but also the forceful sway of the ruler. *Kratos* is supremacy, the superior force. That these forces were at one time invested with religious awe is indicated by certain formulas: Alcinous, for example, is called the "force of Alcinous," compare also *biē Hēraklēeiē* [night of Heracles] and *hierē is Tēlemachoio* [strength of Telemachus]. These idioms are difficult to resolve because they have already by Homer's time become fixed and rigid, nor are we in a position to find out whether *biē* was the original term, or *is* or *menos*. In all probability metrical considerations have played their part in the choice. A proper name such as Telemachus or Alcinous cannot appear in the nominative case at the place which is usually preferred for the citation of proper names, viz., the end of the verse; and so the poet resorts to circumlocution. It has also been observed that adjectival formulas of the type of *biē Hēraklēeiē* occur in connexion with those names which are not members of the Trojan circle; hence it seems fair to conclude that they were adopted from earlier epics. But since they must have been meaningful at one time or another, it has been suggested that among the so-called primitive peoples the king or the priest is often regarded as the possessor of a special magical force which elevates him high above the rest of his fellow tribesmen, and that the formulas which we have cited originally described the leaders as invested with such a force. This is a felicitous suggestion; we would, of course, be mistaken to look for a belief of this sort in our Homeric poems. The very fact that the formulas have become hardened, that metrical patterns now determine their use, prevents us from exploiting them toward a "magic" interpretation of the epic poets. The *Iliad* and the *Odyssey* have a great deal to say about forces, but there is not a scrap of evidence to suggest that there is anything mystic about them; all in all magic and witchcraft have left few traces in the poems, except for some rather atrophied survivals. Homeric man has not yet awakened to the fact that he possesses in his own soul the source of his powers, but neither does he attach the forces to his person by means of magical practices; he receives them as a natural and fitting donation from the gods.

No doubt in the days before Homer magic and sorcery held the field, and even Homer's view of the human soul has its roots in such a "magic" stratum. For it is only too obvious that psychic organs such as the *noos* and the *thymos,* incapable as they are of spontaneous thought or action, are at the mercy of wizardry, and that men who interpret their own mental processes along these lines consider themselves a battleground of arbitrary forces and uncanny powers. This enables us to form some vague opinions about the views which men held concerning themselves and their lives in the pre-Homeric period. The heroes of the *Iliad,* however, no longer feel that they are the playthings of irrational forces; they acknowledge their Olympian gods who constitute a well-ordered and meaningful world. The more the Greeks begin to understand themselves, the more they adopt of this Olympian world and, so to speak, infuse its laws into the human mind. It is true that they continued throughout to preserve a belief in magic, but all those who helped to advance the new era had as little regard for it as Homer, for they pursued the path which Homer had trod. However primitive man's understanding of himself as presented in Homer's speech may appear to us, it also points far into the future: it is the first stage of European thinking.

The Homeric State of Mind

Eric A. Havelock

Poetry, with its rhythms, imagery, and idiom, has in Western Europe been prized and practised as a special kind of experience. Viewed in relation to the day's work, the poetic frame of mind is esoteric, and needs artificial cultivation. Over against it there exists the secular cultural situation, which consists of the thought forms and verbal idiom employed in common transactions, in "affairs" of all kinds. The poetic and the prosaic stand as modes of self-expression which are mutually exclusive. The one is recreation or inspiration, the other is operational. One does not burst into verse in order to admonish one's children, or dictate a letter, or tell a joke, still less to give orders or draft directives.

But in the Greek situation, during the nonliterate epoch, you might do just that. At least, the gulf between poetic and prosaic could not subsist to the degree it does with us. The whole memory of a people was poetised, and this exercised a constant control over the ways in which they expressed themselves in casual speech. The consequences would go deeper than mere queerness or quaintness (from our standpoint) of verbal idiom. They reach into the problem of the character of the Greek consciousness itself, in a given historical period, the kind of thoughts a Greek could think, and the kind he would not think. The Homeric state of mind was, it will appear, something like a total state of mind.

The argument runs somewhat as follows. In any culture, one discerns two areas of communication: (a) there is the casual and ephemeral converse

From *Preface to Plato*. © 1963 by the President and Fellows of Harvard College. The Universal Library, Grosset & Dunlop, 1967.

of daily transaction and (b) there is the area of preserved communication, which means significant communication, which in our culture means "literature," using the word not in an esoteric sense, but to describe the range of experience preserved in books and writings of all kinds, where the ethos and the technology of the culture is preserved. Now, we tend to assume that area (a), being that of the common speech of men, is fundamental, while area (b) is derived from it. But the relationship can be stated in reverse. The idiom and content of area (b), the preserved word, set the formal limits within which the ephemeral word can be expressed. For in area (b) is found the maximum sophistication of which a given epoch is capable. In short, the books and the bookish tradition of a literate culture set the thought-forms of that culture, and either limit or extend them. Mediaeval scholasticism on the one hand, and modern scientific thought on the other, furnish examples of this law.

In an oral culture, permanent and preserved communication is represented in the saga and its affiliates and only in them. These represent the maximum degree of sophistication. Homer, so far from being "special," embodies the ruling state of mind. The casual idiom of his epoch which we have lost should not be assumed to represent a wider and richer range of expression and thought, within which the Homeric vision of the world has formed itself on a special "poetic" basis. On the contrary, it is only in preserved and significant speech, with a life of its own, that the maximum of meaning possible to a cultural state of mind is developed. Epic, despite its slightly esoteric vocabulary (actually, because of this vocabulary), represented significant speech, and it had no prosaic competitor. The Homeric state of mind was therefore, it could be said, the general state of mind.

The truth of this cannot of course be documented from Homer's own day, which was nonliterate, but it can perhaps receive indirect illustration if we turn to those pre-Homeric cultures of the Near East which employed writing systems. These syllabaries were too clumsy and ambiguous to allow fluency or encourage general literacy. Hence their idiom had no power to change the general idiom of oral communication, but on the contrary was forced to reproduce it, and in these transcriptions we get glimpses of that kind of secular converse which in a wholly nonliterate situation like the Greek was not preservable so far as it did not get into the saga.

The tablets found at Knossos and Pylos represent communications of the Myceno-Cretan and Mycenaean cultures. Their decipherment seems to indicate that at the courts of Greek-speaking kings not only inventories but operational directives could be committed to writing. Some scholars have discerned in these directives a Greek that is rhythmical. If they are right, it is possible to conclude that the directive shaped itself in the ear, not in the vision. It was framed orally for verbal memorisation and transmission, and then happened to get written down. The laws of its composition are acoustic, and the script, instead of being used to create the possibilities of prose, remains a servant of the dominant oral technique.

There is a less disputable example. The tablets of Assyria and of Ugarit preserve royal correspondence the idiom of which one would expect to be prosaic, since preservation and transmission are guaranteed by the existence of the visible tablet. It can, after all, be carried from one place to another. Memorisation need not come into question to make the technique of communication effective.

But we find repeatedly in these letters not only the rhythms of poetic speech but the familiar formulaic devices of oral technique—the ring form, the repetition with speakers changed, and similar devices which all at bottom utilise the principle of the echo. Historians, unconsciously misled by modern mental habits, have concluded that this is a ceremonious epistolary style, the rhythms of which have affected poetry, meaning by poetry in this instance the epics, which also exist in the tablets and which exhibit corresponding metrical effects. This exactly reverses the chain of cause and effect. All preserved communication in this culture was orally shaped; if it happened to get written down, the device of script was simply placed at the service of preserving visually what had already been shaped for preservation orally.

The point is of cardinal importance for understanding the progress of Greek letters after Homer. The alphabet proved so much more effective and powerful an instrument for the preservation of fluent communication than any syllabary had been. And by the fourth century its victory was nearly complete, meaning that the original functional purpose of the poetic style was becoming obsolete. You no longer needed to use it to guarantee a life for what was said. But effective as the alphabet was to prove, its functional victory was slow. Down to Euripides (to repeat what has been said earlier) it was still very largely used (aside of course from inscriptions) for the transcription of communication that had in the first place been composed not by the eye but by the ear and composed for recital rather than for reading. The writers of Greece, to repeat, remained under audience-control. That is why they are mostly poets but also poets of a very special kind. Is it worth adding that poets who composed actively till beyond the age of eighty could never in the absence of effective eye glasses have been writers? They must always have dictated to amanuenses.

Continually, as the modern mind strives to come to terms with the mind of archaic and classical Greece, it stumbles over this obstacle to under-standing and reverses the priorities of cause and effect. Thus, the naviga-tional directives in the first book of the *Iliad,* which we have earlier pro-posed as a sample of rhythmically preserved *paideia,* have been understood as a metrical version of an original which was laconic and prosaic; that is, we think in terms of an original which if functional must have been prosaic and which then became poetised for specifically poetic purposes. This inter-prets the Homeric culture in terms of our own, and stands it upside down. In the Homeric, there was no prose original. You framed directives poet-ically or they were no good as directives. Even a catalogue of armour would in its inception and original substance be rhythmic.

In short, all significant communication without exception was framed to obey the psychological laws of the goddess Mnemosune. This brings us to suggest that Homer and Hesiod should be accepted in the first instance not as "poets" in the precious sense of that term but as representing a whole state of the Greek mind. In their formulaic style and their visual imagery and the like they were not behaving as a special sort of person, inspired and "gifted." They were speaking in the only idiom of which their whole culture was capable. The point may be illustrated from an incident which is reported to have occurred during the Gallipoli campaign in 1914–15. A series of mass charges by the Turkish soldiers upon the Allied positions had resulted only in wholesale slaughter. Moral exhaustion and sanitary neces-sities prompted the negotiation of a truce to bury the dead of both sides. The arrangements were concluded only under the most tense psychological conditions. Officers were alert, sentinels kept their finger on the trigger, while friend and foe met in no man's land. As the working parties carried out their grim task under a hot sun in unbelievable stench, tension among the common soldiers somewhat relaxed, and when the operation, governed by split-second timing, came to an end, the two sides before resuming hostilities exchanged greetings and farewells:

> At four o'clock the Turks near Quinn's post came to Herbert for their final orders since none of their own officers were about. He first sent back the grave diggers to their own trenches and at seven minutes past four retired the men who were carrying the white flag. He then walked over to the Turkish trenches to say goodbye. When he remarked to the enemy soldiers there that they would probably shoot him on the following day, they an-swered in a horrified chorus, God forbid. Seeing Herbert stand-ing there groups of Australians came up to the Turks to shake

hands and say goodbye: "Goodbye, old chap; good luck." The Turks answered with one of their proverbs: "Smiling may you go and smiling may you come again."

Here briefly, in an hour of crisis, a semiliterate and a literate culture confronted each other. Each as it speaks under stress resorts to its fundamental idiom of communication. For the one this is laconic and casual prose; for the other it is the rhythm and parallelism of the shaped and preserved formula.

These were not just competing linguistic idioms, English and Turkish. Rather, the British were confronting a foreign state of mind, though one equally effective for its operational purposes. It is to be guessed that the products of modern Turkish literacy in a similar situation would not speak now as their fathers did then on that May afternoon of 1915. It is characteristic of a literate culture that if it is ever confronted with the habit patterns of a nonliterate culture it tends to underestimate their efficiency. The Turkish soldiers of this same campaign were accompanied in their trenches by the Imams who chanted exhortations and the like before battle. To their British opponents, it looked at first like a nonmilitary obstacle to efficiency, a piece of backward superstition. They learnt differently. In fact, it was a functional application of the oral technique to military discipline and morale, among a soldiery who did not read.

The ways of war bring to the surface the essential mechanisms of a culture complex. The chain of command, always there beneath the surface in civil life, holding the society together, is in warfare exposed in its most essential forms. T. E. Lawrence, describing the muster of an expeditionary force of Arab warriors, observed the improvised verses which accompanied the line-up, and the rhythms which assisted the organisation of the forward march. These procedures were not the result of some special addiction to heroism on the part of the Arabs; they were not Homeric in our narrow and emasculated sense, meaning simply romantic. Rather they were truly Homeric in their functional necessity. Here was a culture, strictly nonliterate, as the Balkan cultures were not. The epic style was therefore a necessity for government and not just a means of recreation. Lawrence also noticed the educational system centred on the hearth by which this epic capacity was indoctrinated. Presumably, as Arabia Deserta succumbs to literacy, these mechanisms will wither away. Only a few ballad-makers will survive, a vestigial remnant divorced from functional relationship to their community, and waiting for antiquarians to collect their songs under the impression that this is truly Homeric stuff.

In such nonliterate cultures the task of education could be described as putting the whole community into a formulaic state of mind. The instrument for doing this was to use the tribal epics as a paradigm. Their style is intensified to be sure. Their idiom shows a virtuosity which in common transactions might be imitated but at a simpler level of artistry. A minstrel would be a man of superior memory, and so also might be the prince and the judge. This automatically meant superior rhythmic sense, since rhythm was the preservative of speech. With superior memory and rhythmic sense would go also a greater virtuosity in the management of the formulas. The lesser memories of the populace would be content to use simpler and less elaborate language. But the whole community from minstrel and prince down to the peasant was attuned to the psychology of remembrance.

An epic might memorialise a whole area of history and manners. In a village the local head-men might be able to repeat it, the peasantry might remember only part of it. But all alike were trained to respond to formulaic directives—a military order, let us say, or a local tax assessment—in which the epic style was imitated or echoed.

This amounts to saying that the poet, and particularly the epic poet, would exercise a degree of cultural control over his community which is scarcely imaginable under modern literate conditions in which poetry is no longer part of the day's work. His epic language would constitute a kind of culture language, a frame of reference and a standard of expression to which in varying degree all members of the community were drawn. In our own culture of writers and readers the existing body of prose literature performs this same function for the common members of the language group. Their speech habits will vary in range and cultivation but in general these habits betray a relationship to the written literature, which has been described by one authority as follows:

> More important than the writing itself is the written tradition. In a culture language this exerts itself upon all levels, dictating words, formations and turns of phrase and constantly introducing into the spoken tongue echoes of the study, the church, and the technical and learned professions . . . all parts of a culture language may suffer this influence; phonemics through the introduction of foreign words pronounced with foreign sounds, morphology and syntax through the retention or revival of devices taken from literature. The entire question of stylistics is vitally affected by the interplay of the written tradition and the spoken tongue . . . the quotation, the set phrase, the technical expression and in general the construction modelled upon the

> written language are everday phenomena in such a language. It
> is in fact not too much of an over-statement to say that the re-
> sources of literature constitute a blank cheque which the speaker
> in speaking can fill in to almost any amount.

The term "culture language" as used in this quotation has been restricted to
languages which have a written literature. The theory can be supplemented
by the assumption that in a society of oral preservation it is therefore the
epic, in the main, which provides the culture language. The extent of its
role in this regard will depend on the degree of virtuosity which is used to
endow speech with survival power. The more contrived and elaborate the
devices that are used, the longer is the life possessed by the speech thus
shaped. If the written literature of a modern culture is able to exercise over
common idiom that indirect control which is described in our quotation,
this is because it has a longer life than the common speech possesses. In a
sense it has discovered the secret of making the word immortal, in so far as
the symbols on the page can be kept and copied and repeated in unchanged
form, theoretically forever. So we are continually reminded as we read, that
this, the written word, is more honorific than our casual utterance, and we
are drawn unconsciously to accept it as a paradigm of usage, to which we
expect to approximate but no more.

The Homeric epics constituted a body of invisible writing imprinted
upon the brain of the community. They represented a monopoly exercised
by the epic technique over the culture language. Such control had to be
linked with functional performance to be effective. The fact that the Homeric was not the vernacular tongue only heightened its power of control.
The precise times and conditions under which the Greek vernaculars separated themselves out are still obscure. But throughout archaic and classical
Greece you still said things Homerically and tended to think things Homerically. Here was not just a poetic style but an international one, a superior idiom of communication.

Control over the style of a people's speech, however indirect, means
control also over their thought. The two technologies of preserved communication known to man, namely the poetised style with its acoustic
apparatus and the visual prosaic style with its visual and material apparatus,
each within their respective domains control also the content of what is
communicable. Under one set of conditions man arranges his experience in
words in some one given way; under the second set of conditions he arranges the same experience differently in different words and with different
syntax and perhaps as he does so the experience itself changes. This

amounts to saying that the patterns of his thought have historically run in two distinct grooves, the oral and the written. The case for this assumption has not yet been clarified. But at least Plato, if we may now return to him, seems to have been convinced that poetry and the poet had exercised a control not merely over Greek verbal idiom but over the Greek state of mind and consciousness. The control in his view had been central and he describes it as though it were monopolistic. This agrees with our own analysis of the poet's situation in the Greek Dark Age. If Plato is correct, this situation had continued virtually unchanged through classical Greece.

Nature and Culture in the *Iliad*: Purification

James M. Redfield

Psuchē and Noos

Wittgenstein wrote, in *Tractatus Logico-Philosophicus,* "At death the world does not alter; it ceases. Death is not an event of life. No one lives through his death." This very modern formulation recovers the archaic Homeric understanding. Death is not a problem for the Homeric hero; his death concludes his story and completes his fate. The dead hero is a problem for others, for those who must live with the fact of his absence; death is a problem for the hero himself only to the degree that he feels himself one with those others. Thus when Hector speaks to Andromache of his own death, he speaks only of those others, of the fall of the city and his wife's slavery:

> And one will say, who sees your flowing tears:
> "That is Hector's wife; he was best at fighting
> Of the Trojan horsemen who fought before Ilium."
> Thus he will say, and thus renew your pain,
> Widowed of your man who kept you from bondage.
> May the grave mound hide me, dead beneath the earth,
> Before I hear your cry, and you're dragged away.
> (bk. 6, ll. 459–65)

Hector's wish is to be absent from the events he foresees; he therefore

---

From *Nature and Culture in the* Iliad: *The Tragedy of Hector.* © 1975 by the University of Chicago. University of Chicago Press, 1975.

thinks of himself not only as dead but as properly buried. By the funeral, the others who survive the dead man mark the fact of his death and assert his absence. The funeral is the *geras* of the dead (bk. 16, ll. 457 and 675); *geras* is the name for those marks of honor which a man is entitled to claim in virtue of his status or social role. In one sense the *geras* marks the status; in another sense it confers status, so that the loss of *geras* (as in the case of Chryseis or Briseis) threatens a loss of status. The funeral may thus be thought of as a ceremony by which a definite social status is conferred upon the dead. In the funeral the community declares that the dead man is gone and that life continues without him. He has done what he could, and his community declares that it can expect nothing more of him. Since he can no longer be among them, he is entitled to the status of the departed. They thus release him. It is this release for which the *psuchai* pray when, during the interval between death and burial, they speak to the living. The *psuchē*, I shall now suggest, survives death as a consequence of the fact that man dies not only organically but also socially, dies not only to nature but to culture.

Homer is pre-Cartesian and, for that matter, pre-Socratic. He does not make a sharp distinction between body and soul. But he does, in his own way, make a sharp distinction between theory and practice. It is the distinction we must understand if we are to understand the *psuchē*.

The notion of life which centers on the *menos, phrenes,* and *thumos* is a notion of life centering on action; the live creature has a source of motion within himself and sets his own direction. There is, however, another notion of life in the poems, by which life is associated with vision. We are reminded that fire has a double meaning; it is both heat and light, the source of both motion and vision.

Associated with vision is *noos*. One is said to *noēsai* with the eyes (see, e.g., bk. 15, l. 422). *Noos* is, however, different from sight: Sarpedon says he cannot *ideein* the Trojans or *noēsai* them either (bk. 5, l. 475); he does not see them or notice them anywhere. It is the *noos* which catches a signal, as when Ajax nods to Phoenix, and *noēse . . . Odusseus* (bk. 9, l. 223). The tripods of Hephaestus have a *noos*; they can take instructions (bk. 18, ll. 419–20). When Eurycleia recognizes the scar, Penelope fails to notice, for "Athena turned aside her *noos*" (*Odyssey,* bk. 19, l. 479). *Noos* is linked to recognition and responsive understanding: we might say that vision takes in the look of a thing, *noos* its meaning. *Ideein* and *noēsai* are not, therefore, two separate acts; rather, the *noos* further forms perceiving consciousness so that what is perceived is a world of recognized meanings.

Noos is not always linked to perception; one is said to *noēsai* "with the eyes" only in those cases in which the direct experience of the knower is stressed. *Noos* is also connected with words; it is a source of *muthoi*. The unspoken word is concealed in the *noos* (bk. 1, l. 363). A *noēma* is a plan or intention. But these uses also are linked to concrete picturings, not in the mode of direct perception, but in the secondary mode of imagination (bk. 16, ll. 80–83). The planner *sees* a future situation and uses words to describe it. *Noos* has to do with plans or intentions because these are themselves a kind of anticipatory vision. Thus it is said that Zeus "does not bring to pass all the *noēmata* of men" (bk. 18, l. 328; cf. bk. 23, l. 149). Man imagines a future, but it does not come to pass (bk. 10, l. 104).

As the recognition of meaning in things perceived or imagined, *noos* is a theoretical faculty. Whereas *thumos* is the consciousness which the organism has of itself in the world, *noos* is consciousness of the world in which the organism is. The objects of recognition are out there: persons, things, and events which are separate from ourselves. *Noos* perceives what is so, what the facts mean, and is in this sense dispassionate. Yet *noos* is a source of passionate excitement. "In all those cases in which the verb *noein* has a direct and concrete object violent emotion is caused by the *noein*." Meaning is *to us,* and the perceived meaning is expressed by the state of the organism. *Noos* is thus, like *thumos,* located in the *stēthos; noos* may be thought of as a further forming of *thumos.* "It is not identical in meaning with *thumos* but is rather something in, a defining of, this as e.g. a current in a sense consists of but defines, controls, air or water." Thus even knowledge or vision can be said to be in the *phrenes* or *thumos* when the thing known or seen has some immediate practical or affective relevance (bk. 21, l. 61; *Odyssey,* bk. 8, l. 45).

Noos is thus a theoretical faculty which has to do with particulars— particulars in two senses. In the first place, *noos* grasps meaning immediately; the act, *noein,* may follow a period of attention or puzzlement, but the clarity, when it comes, comes with the immediacy of vision. "In Homer *nous* never means 'reason' and *noein* never 'to reason,' whether inductively or deductively." Second, *noos* grasps the meaning which its objects have for the particular knower; thus the *nooi* of different men and of men in different societies differ (*Odyssey,* bk. 1, l. 3). *Noos* does not discover some universal pattern of meaning or eternal truth; rather, it is the faculty by which we discern meaning as we happen to discern it.

The duality of *thumos* and *noos* is thus not based on a distinction between emotion and reason or on a distinction between the particular and the universal. It is based rather on a distinction between the inner and the outer, between the expression of ourselves in the world and the impression the world makes on us. *Noos* is a kind of metaperception. It is a receptivity to meaning and as such is passive; there is no *menos* in *noos. Thumos* always involves intention or inclination and thus the active power of the organism to affect its environment; *noos* may involve mere recognition. Thus when Eurypolus is retiring, wounded, from the battle, Patroclus meets him and speaks with him, and "his *noos* at least was still *empedos*" (bk. 11, l. 813). Eurypolus's strength has been subdued by the wound, but he is still conscious and rational; one can talk with him. The connection previously noted between *noos* and language, counsel and planning, helps to explain the fact that, while *thumos* exists also in animals, *noos* is specific to man. It should therefore have some relation to the man-specific soul, the *psuchē*.

The *psuchē* is the eschatological soul; it does nothing except depart from a man when he dies—or is close to death. The *psuchai* of the living are spoken of only as something that is kept in life and lost in death. *Psuchē*, unlike the other souls of which we have been speaking, is not a functioning of the organism or a locus of experience.

It has long been noticed that, in several passages in Homer, when a hero faints, his *psuchē* passes from him, but that when he revives, it is not said to return; rather, his *thumos* returns and "collects itself within him." This, I would suggest, is because unconsciousness, like death, is not an experience. When the man revives, he "comes to himself"; as long as he is unconscious, he exists only for others. The *psuchē*, I wish to assert, is a self that exists for others, one aspect of the social soul.

Menos, as we saw, is a formed process of matter; *thumos* is a further forming of *menos*, and *noos* of *thumos*. As all of these things are functionings of one another, they are all equally mortal. *Noos*, since it is particular and of particulars, has none of the special standing of the Aristotelian *nous*—which latter is, in a sense, immortal, in that its principle is universal and therefore eternal. In the Homeric picture, rather, some element of the man survives death not because man has *noos* but because he is in life the object of *noos*. The *noos* of others has recognized him and has thus given him a social identity and a proper name.

A proper name is the concept of a particular person; beings with proper names are recognizable, not merely as members of a species but as irreducibly distinct individuals. Proper names are conferred by men on creatures and things—on domestic animals, for instance, and places—insofar as those things are included within the fabric of society. But most creatures and things remain nameless. Human beings, the social creatures par excellence, are the only beings (except possibly gods) to whom a name is of the essence:

> No one is quite nameless among men,
> Neither low nor high, from the moment he is born.
> (*Odyssey*, bk. 8, ll. 552–53)

To the proper name—the concept of the individual—corresponds a material fact: his personal appearance. It is by his looks that we recognize him. Because every man has a distinctive appearance, he can be the object of *noos*. As the name is the identity of the man in an ideal sense, his appearance is his identity in a material sense.

At the moment of death the man ceases to function; he is no longer a source of help or harm. But his identity persists. The man is gone, but two new things come into existence—or, we might better say, come to our attention. One is the *sōma* or corpse. The *sōma* is inert matter, organism without *menos*. As it is no longer self-maintaining, its appearance begins to change. The other is the *psuchē*. The *psuchē* is an *eidōlon,* an image; it looks "wonderfully like the man," but "there is no *phrēn* in it at all (bk. 23, ll. 103–7). The *psuchē* is immaterial (it cannot be touched) and had no *menos*; it can speak only in dreams or if provided with a quasi-*menos* by being fed hot blood. The *psuchē* is the recognizable appearance of the man, his concrete identity. If we remember that we are speaking within the realm of the particular, we shall be correct to say that at the moment of death man is divided into matter and form—particular matter and particular form. Thus we understand why, while the seat of consciousness is the *stēthos*, the *psuchē* is particularly associated with the head and also with the *rhethea,* an old word apparently meaning "face." The head and the face are the most recognizable parts of the person; if his identity is specially located in any part of him, it must be there.

The dead are *amenēna karēna,* "heads without *menos*." Their identity survives, but without power, and they are located somewhere else, in the most distant, dark, unknowable realm. All this objectifies the view of death we noticed earlier: that death is an experience of the living, for whom the dead man survives in the modality of his absence. His face haunts the memory of those who must live without him. The *psuchai* in the house of Hades are precisely the absent ones; the funeral is the ceremony of their departure and the ritual of their release.

The division of the dead person into *psuchē* and *sōma* marks his disintegration into natural and cultural aspects. The Homeric funeral deals with the fact of death in both these aspects.

AFTER DEATH

A dead body is a puzzle. It is everything the person ever was and yet is nothing like him; in death he is the same and yet opposite to what he was in life. The dead warrior comes into the hands of his women; he who has been so long their protection becomes their task. It is almost impossible to believe that this familiar being is no longer a person; thus Achilles in his farewell to the dead Patroclus puts his hands on the *stēthos* of the corpse, as if by sheer force he could reach the consciousness which is no longer there to hear his words (bk. 18, l. 317 and bk. 23, l. 18). The living are reluctant to relinquish their dead; it is the dead Patroclus who is ready to depart.

Yet the dead body begins to rot. Once the *psuchē* is gone, the familiar form begins to turn into something else as it blends into the flux of nature. This is the horror of dead bodies; they are interstitial things, for in death the whole person becomes a kind of excrement, the mere remains of life. To this puzzle there are at least two solutions. One, embalming, was the solution of the Mycenaeans; by this practice the last indignity of death is avoided. The body is preserved, and it may even be held to continue a kind of limited life in its house beneath the ground. Traces of this practice may survive in Homer, but the Homeric solution takes the opposite course. The body is washed, oiled, purified, if wounded, with flour (bk. 18, ll. 350–53 and *Odyssey*, bk. 24, ll. 43–45), and shrouded; it is, as it were, cleaned and packaged and thus marked off from nature. It is then burnt. That which had been sustained by the organic *menos* is now handed over to pure *menos* and destroyed. Whereas rotting is unclean, burning is clean; the thing that rots becomes something formless, whereas the thing burnt ceases to exist altogether. To be nothing is an absolute condition and thus is a kind of form; the burnt corpse has been spared decay. The bones persist, because the Homeric fire of wood and suet was not hot enough to burn them; they are in a sense embalmed, as they are folded in layers of fat, placed in a golden vessel, and buried deep, with heavy stones above them, where it is hoped no change of place or state will ever come to them (bk. 22, ll. 238–57, bk. 24, ll. 792–98).

The fire is one half of the funeral, the half that deals with the dead organism. The other half deals with the departed as a social identity, and from this point of view the funeral is a long farewell. The dead man is thought of as someone going away on a journey; the things and creatures burnt with Patroclus are spoken of as "all that is fitting for the corpse to have in his journey to the misty dark" (bk. 23, ll. 50–51, cf. 137). The formal laments, the *gooi,* do not speak of the dead man as he was in life; rather they speak of how things are now that he is gone, the difference made by his absence. Mourning is not so much memory of the past as a definition of the new situation; mourning thus looks forward to the situation beyond the funeral and celebrates the departed, not for what he did, but for how much he will be missed. The living person is thus dismissed, and a new social figure, the absent one, is created. At the close of the ceremony this negative figure is immortalized by the *sēma,* which is set up for "men-to-come to inquire about" (*Odyssey,* bk. 11, l. 76; cf. bk. 7, ll. 89–91, *Odyssey,* bk. 4, l. 584, *Odyssey,* bk. 24, ll. 80–84).

The *sēma* is *empedon;* a *sēma* is mentioned in a simile as the typically *empedon* thing (bk. 17, ll. 434–36). The man who is dead to others survives as a name and a history. He will provoke the question: Who is it that is dead?—and to this question men will for a while be able to provide an answer. The *sēma* on earth mirrors the *psuchē* in the house of Hades; both are permanent impotent markers of the identity that is gone. The *psuchai* in Hades survive, in a sense, but they survive in an inert condition. They have no adventures after death. Even in the *Odyssey,* where Odysseus can evoke the *psuchai* by a magical procedure and where the conversations of the dead among themselves are recorded, the world of the *psuchai* is not thought of as a world of experience but of memory. The dead tell each other the events of their lives, and that is all. One recently dead may be thought of as a messenger from the living; otherwise, the dead have no knowledge of events after their own death. They are hungry for news of the living (*Odyssey,* book 11, ll. 457–64, 492–540). Anticleia can give Odysseus news of Ithaca only because, having died since his departure, she has been there more recently than he has. In life the *psuchē* is not a locus of experience, and in death it is incapable of experience or change. So the existence of the *psuchē* in Hades is not a continuation of the personal life but rather a kind of monument to the fact that personal life once existed.

The prayer of the *psuchē* before the body's burial is thus not really a prayer for admission to another world; the house of Hades is a world only in a very limited sense. The *psuchē* prays for release from this world, which may be thought of as admission to an antiworld. Hades is lord of one-third of the inheritance of Cronos, but he is "loathed of gods and men," and his realm lies beyond the ocean stream (*Odyssey,* bk. 11, ll. 155–59)—which is to say, outside the world. His world is a nonworld. Similarly, the funeral is a conversion of the person into a nonperson, into the negative of a person. The body is spared decay by being annihilated. The social person is spared social weakness—unfulfilled responsibilities, unrealizable wishes—by being converted from an active person into a remembered and remembering person. In both senses the funeral purifies the dead man by setting a definite period to his existence and converting him into something not subject to change.

For the living, the funeral is a ceremony of parting; the dead depart, and the living take their leave of them. Since, in community, we are one with one another—especially with those to whom we are bound by love or kinship—this parting also tears at the mourner, who, in parting with the dead, parts with a part of himself. This thought leads to an interpretation of the shearing of the hair.

Between death and burning, the dead person is in a liminal condition; he is neither alive nor properly dead. He is decaying, yet he is clung to; his mourners thus enter the liminal realm with him. They share his death and bring on themselves an image of death's befoulment by pouring ashes over themselves, tearing their hair and cheeks, rolling in the dung, and throwing off their clothes. The dead man is going on a journey, and the impulse of the mourners is to go with him; the most perfect mourning would be suicide, and this is treated as a real possibility (bk. 18, l. 34). Short of this the mourner may suspend his life, as Achilles abstains from food, sleep, washing, and the act of love (bk. 24, ll. 129–31). The time of mourning is the last time together for the dead and the living, who share some condition between life and death. This sharing is enacted by the funeral feast of the Myrmidons, which is held by the corpse of Patroclus; the mourners eat the meat of the sacrificial animals, while the blood is poured around the corpse in a ceremony of feeding the *psuchē* (bk. 23, l. 34).

The shearing of the hair, I suggest, has to do with this common liminality of corpse and mourner. The hair (along with the nails) is unique among body parts in that it grows and yet is inert and can be lost without pain or injury. Furthermore, the hair continues to grow after death. Hair is thus part of us without quite being a part, and has a kind of life of its own; its life is a metonym of our life. When Achilles left Phthia for Troy, Peleus vowed that Achilles would keep his hair uncut and on his return would cut it and dedicate it to the river Spercheius. He thus vowed that, if Achilles brought his (actual) life back to his own soil, his (metaphorical) life would be given to the river; life would be paid for life. At Patroclus's funeral Achilles breaks this vow, cuts his hair, and puts it in Patroclus's hands on the pyre. By sending his life to the fire with the body of his friend (bk. 24, ll. 144–51), Achilles gives up his hope of returning to Phthia alive; he (metaphorically) dies with Patroclus, just as he later expects (actually) to die at Troy and be buried with Patroclus (bk. 23, ll. 245–48).

Achilles' act is a more elaborate version of the ordinary ritual of mourning, in which the mourner places a lock of his hair on the body to be burnt (bk. 23, ll. 134–36). Achilles' explanation of his act can guide us in our understanding of the more ordinary ritual. The mourner, placed between the living and the dead, splits himself in two; he gives a part or a version of his life to the dead man and thus asserts his solidarity with him. The mourner is then free to turn back and reassert his solidarity with the living. As the funeral releases the dead to death, so also it releases the living to life (cf. bk. 23, ll. 52–53).

The death of a man inflicts a wound on the community. One point on the social network ceases to respond to the gifts and demands of the others. Furthermore, as the body of the dead man begins to rot, the whole social body, of which he had been a part, becomes vulnerable to the processes of nature. The dead man still engages the affections of his mourners, but he is turning into something else. The threat of deformation, formlessness, and impurity, therefore, is not local to the dead man; it affects all bound to him in ties of community.

The funeral pyre cauterizes and heals this wound. At the same time, through mourning and memorial, the social fabric is reconstructed in a new form which takes account of the absence of this member. In the funeral the community acts on its own behalf to reassert its own continuity in spite of the disorderly forces which assail it. By the funeral the community purifies itself. . . .

The Ransoming of Hector

We now turn to the ransoming of Hector and the final purification of the *Iliad,* achieved not by the reconstruction of the human community but by the separation of the hero from the community. The end of the *Iliad* is a ceremonial recognition of the monstrous singularity of Achilles.

At the beginning of book 24, we find that for Achilles nothing has changed. These ceremonies are for him inefficacious; they leave him exactly where he was:

> The games were dissolved; the folk went back to their ships
> And scattered. Then they turned their minds to food
> And the fullness of sweet sleep. Achilles alone
> Wept; he remembered his friend, nor ever did sleep
> Come, that subdues us all, but he turned and turned
> In desire for Patroclus' manhood and vivid strength,
> For all he'd traversed with him, the pains they'd suffered
> In wars of men and in crossing the painful waves.
> As he remembered, the tears welled up in him hot;
> On his side he lay for a while, and then for a while
> On his back, then face down. Then he got up
> And twisted grieving, along the shore. Nor did dawn
> Find him unmindful, shining on sea and shore,
> But whenever he had yoked swift horses to their car

He tied to it Hector for dragging behind the wheels;
Thrice he would drag him around Patroclus' tomb;
Then he would rest in the hut and leave him there,
Stretched face down in the dust. From Hector, Apollo
Kept off despoilment, in pity for his flesh,
Dead though he was. He covered him with the aegis
Of gold, so that the dragging would not tear him.
Thus Achilles despoiled bright Hector in his raging.

(bk. 24, ll. 1–22)

In this way the poet sets before us the problem of his final book. Hector
and Achilles have descended together into an impure world, a world beyond the reach of ceremonies. For Hector this descent has been into power-
lessness, for Achilles into mere power, power without meaning. Achilles
enacts and reenacts his conquest of Hector; he cannot even destroy the
body, which thus remains an eternal object of his malice. The two heroes
are locked together in an everlasting dance of hatred—despoiler and victim,
predator and prey.

If this conflict is to be resolved, it must be shifted to a level on which
resolution is possible. The war at Troy is a conflict between two human
communities, but it is also a conflict within a community, the community
of the gods. Within this divine community the conflict can be resolved, and
it is, in three swift speeches: statement, counterstatement, and an arbitration
by the king:

There spoke among the immortals then Phoebus Apollo:
"You are harsh, gods, malicious; don't you remember
Hector burning the thighs of oxen and goats?
You'll take no step, corpse though he is, to save him,
To where his wife could see him, his mother, his child,
His father Priam, all his folk, who'd quickly
Kindle his pyre and burn his possessions around him.
But destroyer Achilles, gods, has all your help,
Whose heart knows nothing proper, nor is his mind
Responsive within. He thinks like a savage lion
Whose strength is great, who yields to his prideful heart
And springs on the flocks of men, to seize his dinner.
So Achilles destroyed all pity, nor is aidōs
His, which surely despoils men and maintains them.
Men can lose those even closer to them—
Even a whole brother, perhaps, or a son—

Yet when they have wept and mourned, they put it from them,
For the Portioners made the heart of man enduring.
But Hector—after he'd taken his spirit from him—
Slung behind horses, around his own friend's tomb
He drags. It is not fine, nor is it proper.
Superior though he is, we might still feel *nemesis,*
For senseless is the earth he despoils in his raging."
    Then in her anger answered white-armed Hera:
"That is the way *you* say it, silver-bow.
Achilles and Hector, perhaps, you'd make equal in honor.
But Hector is mortal, he suckled a woman's breast.
Achilles is born of a goddess, whom I myself
Reared and nursed, and gave to a man as his wife,
To Peleus, who is heart-close to the immortals.
You all came, gods, to the wedding. You were there too,
Playing your lyre at the feast, faithless, untrusted."
    Then to her, answering, spoke cloud-gathering Zeus:
"Hera, do not spoil with rage at the gods.
In honor they won't be the same. But still, this Hector
Was closest to us of mortals who are in Troy,
Especially to me, since he never spared of my gifts,
My altar was never lacking of fitting feasts,
Of wine and fat-steam. That is our proper privilege.
Let's not think of stealing—it can't be done—
By stealth from Achilles, Hector. She's always there,
His mother, who watches beside him night and day.
So let some one of the gods call Thetis to me
That I may tell her my thought, the way Achilles
Will take the gifts of Priam and ransom Hector."
                                 (bk. 24, ll. 32–76)

    The speech of Apollo is godlike in a sense that is uncharacteristic of the *Iliad.* The gods of the *Iliad,* as we have seen, have been drawn into the action, have become persons within an unfolding plot beyond the control even of Zeus. But Apollo here stands back from the action, from the human world, and prescribes for it. This shift of perspective accounts, perhaps, for the oddities of language in the speech, for example the phrase about *aidōs* as maintainer and despoiler and the reference to the "dumb earth." This is the only place in Homer where the Portioners, the Moirai, are mentioned in the plural, and it is the only place in the *Iliad* where *moira* is called the source of the way things are in general rather than, narrowly, the source of the finitude of life. Perhaps most significant is the fact that this is the only place in the *Iliad* where *nemesis* is used of the attitude of the gods toward human beings who have broken the moral code. Apollo's moralism is close to Phoenix's moralism in book 9; man was meant to be of enduring heart, and Achilles is a transgressor. He, Apollo, is the guarantor of that norm.

This Apollo carries us back to the Apollo of the first book, who sent the plague on those who offended his priest. The appearance of the god in this role—distant from the action rather than part of it—is a sign that the poem is drawing to its conclusion; as the action slackens, the gods disentangle themselves from it. But it is also true that this notion of god as the guarantor of norms is introduced here only to be rejected. Hera protests that Achilles is not human in the ordinary sense; he is a member of the divine community. The gods came to Peleus's wedding; they are joined to Achilles by bonds of kinship and ceremony and cannot simply impose on him the behavior they require.

Zeus agrees with Hera. The notion, circulating a few lines earlier, that Hermes should steal Hector's body, is rejected. Achilles' immortal mother makes such a solution impossible. Rather, Achilles must be drawn into the divine community. Zeus sends for Thetis. As she came to Zeus from her son at the beginning, so he sends her to her son at the end. The social anomaly which was the source of the whole catastrophe becomes the source of the final reconciliation. The action of the poem rounds into completed form.

When Thetis brings Achilles his instructions, he assents in two bare lines:

> So be it. Who brings the ransom will take the corpse,
> If Zeus with thoughtful heart himself instructs me.
> (bk. 24, ll. 139–40)

This compliance should not surprise us; it matches Achilles' compliance to Athena in the first book (bk. 1, ll. 216–18). Achilles never loses his confidence in the gods, aside from one moment of panic in the river (bk. 21, ll. 273–83), and on that occasion his angry prayer is promptly answered (bk. 21, ll. 288–97). Achilles' story grows from his marginal standing between two communities, but the disorder thus generated is all between himself and men. In the human community his standing is (ambiguously) high, and he finds himself baffled; in the divine community his standing is unambiguously low, and with his usual clarity he accepts proper instruction.

The dramatic tension of the last book is not in Achilles' consent but in Priam's journey to Achilles. Priam must be introduced into the semihuman, god-inhabited world where Achilles is at home. Iris comes to Priam and promises him Hermes as escort (bk. 24, ll. 182–83). Hermes in the *Odyssey* is *psuchopompos,* conductor of souls to Hades; here he appears as god of sleep (bk. 24, ll. 343–44, cf. 445). Priam's journey is a kind of dream voyage or descent into the underworld. Priam declares that he is ready to die with his son (bk. 24, ll. 224–27, cf. 246); as he goes to him,

> All his dear ones followed,
> Mourning aloud, as if he were going to death.
> (bk. 24, ll. 327–28)

Priam rejects his wife's appeal, reviles his sons, and goes into the dark.

As Priam separates himself from his own world, he is, in a limited but real sense, included in the divine world. He goes as father to son, and to help him, Zeus sends Hermes, "his own son" (bk. 24, l. 333); Hermes says to Priam, "I think of you as if you were my own father" (bk. 24, l. 371, cf. 398). Father Zeus, that is, sends to father Priam a son to be a son to him. Priam—for the first time in the poem—feels the gods close to him. He says to Hermes:

> Child, it is good and fitting to give gifts to the gods,
> Since never my son—I mean my son that was—
> Forgot in his halls the gods, who hold Olympus;
> So they remembered him, even in death.
> (bk. 24, ll. 425–28)

Before his departure Priam purifies himself with water and pours a libation of wine, praying for an omen, which Zeus sends (bk. 24, ll. 303–21). He commits himself to the gods. Priam and his herald meet Hermes at the river running between the armies; everything is dark and wrapped in mist (bk. 24, ll. 349–51). The journey is a rite of departure and crossing-over. Zeus has contrived a ceremony which takes place outside the human world, and therefore at night and by magic.

Priam's gesture of submission to Achilles is itself a kind of impossible act. He says:

> I've endured such as no man ever endured on the earth:
> To raise to my mouth the hand of my son's killer.
> (bk. 24, ll. 505–6)

The poetry of this gesture is complex:

> Great Priam stood by him close;
> His hands took Achilles' knees; he kissed his hands—
> Dread, man-slaying, which killed his many sons—
> As, when the blindness takes a man, and at home
> He's killed a man, and he comes to another's folk,
> To a rich man's house, and awe takes those who see him,
> So Achilles looked in awe upon godlike Priam.
>
> (bk. 24, ll. 477–83)

By the simile Priam is turned into the slayer and Achilles the rich king—as if, in the eye of the poet, they take on each other's roles for a moment. This likeness is perhaps already there in line 478, which begins with one pair of hands and ends with the other. Achilles' hands are called *androphonos,* man-slaying, both there and when he touches the *stēthos* of the dead Patroclus (bk. 18, l. 317 and bk. 23, l. 18). In both passages there is a contrast between the killing power of the hands and their gentle gesture. But *androphonos* is properly an epithet of warriors, and this is the epithet specific to Hector (occurring eleven times, including bk. 24, l. 509). In kissing Achilles' hands, Priam seems to cross a line, perhaps even to violate a taboo; he caresses the object of his loathing. But the language reminds us that the man-slaying hands slew a manslayer, that Achilles has done nothing to Hector which Hector did not promise Patroclus. This categorical perception of the relation between the parties—by which it is seen that, given different circumstances, each could have been in the place of the other—is the basis of the reconciliation.

Priam speaks to Achilles of Peleus, and Achilles weeps; Priam falls before him, weeping for Hector, and "Achilles wept for his father, and then again for Patroclus" (bk. 24, ll. 511–12). Priam is like Peleus; both are old men, and fathers, and, as Hector died before his father, so will Achilles die before his. When Achilles weeps for Patroclus, however, he shares Priam's mourning differently; both have lost the persons dearest to them, and their pain is common. Achilles sees himself both in Priam and in Hector. The terrible clarity of Achilles' speech to the embassy is not lost but relocated as the point of view shifts. Achilles' rending sense of his own mortality, which in book 9 had isolated him from others, even his friends, here becomes a bond with others, even with his enemy. At the moment Achilles feels himself most a mortal man, he stands away from his men, as the gods do, and sees himself one with other mortals, "like to the breed of leaves." In their common mourning, Achilles and Priam together experience the limiting finitude of the heroic consciousness. This shift of perspective is the subjective content of the ceremony contrived by Zeus between the worlds.

Achilles states this subjective content in two speeches, one before the release of Hector's body, one after:

> Wretch, your heart has had to bear much evil.
> How did you endure to come to the ships alone,
> Before the eyes of a man who your many and good
> Sons has slaughtered? Iron-hard your spirit.
> Come, sit here, and all this pain of ours
> We shall let rest in the heart, although it hurts us.
> There's no conclusion comes to cruel mourning.
> Thus the gods have spun for wretched men,
> To live in pain. But they themselves are carefree.
> Two are the jars set on the floor of Zeus,
> Full of their gifts of evil, and one full of blessings;
> When he mixes his gifts, Zeus who delights in thunder,
> Sometimes it runs to evil, sometimes to good—
> But when his gifts are sorrow, Zeus marks his victim;
> Evil wasting drives him across the earth;
> He wanders, by gods disowned, by mortal men.
> Thus to Peleus gods gave shining gifts
> From birth. All mankind he excelled
> In happiness and wealth; he was king in Phthia,
> And him, though a mortal, gods gave a goddess-wife.
> But then god gave the evil: he'd not have
> A race of mighty sons born in his house.
> One son he had, short-lived; he'll not even have
> My care in his aging, since so far from home
> I sit in Troy, harming you and your sons.
> You also, old man, once, we hear, were happy.
> All far Lesbos holds, the seat of Makar,
> Wide Phrygia, the trackless Hellespont,
> All that, they say, you excelled in wealth and sons.
> But since they brought this sorrow, the Heavenly Ones,
> Ever about your town are war and dying.
> Bear it. Don't weep forever in your heart.
> You'll not conclude it, grieving a fine son,
> Nor bring him back; you'll just add evil to evil.
>   (bk. 24, ll. 518–51)

Your son is ransomed, old man, as you asked;
He lies on the bier. When first light is breaking
You'll see him yours. Now let us think of supper—
For even Niobe remembered to eat,
Although twelve children perished in her house—
Six were daughters, six were full-grown sons.
Apollo killed the boys with his silver bow,
Angry with Niobe; Artemis killed the girls
Because she had likened herself to fair-cheeked Leto:
That Leto's children were two, but she had many.
So those two took her many children from her.
Nine days they lay in gore, nor was anyone there
To bury them; Zeus had turned the folk to stone;
The heavenly gods on the tenth day buried them,
And she remembered to eat, worn out with weeping.
Now in the rocks, on the solitary mountain
In Sipylos, where they say is the lair of nymphs,
Divine girls, who dance by the Achelous,
There, stone though she is, she consumes her sorrow.
But come, we two should also, old man, think
To eat. And later you will mourn your son
When you take him home. He will surely be much wept-for.

(bk. 24, ll. 599–620)

In these two speeches the hero of the *Iliad* states the concluding synthesis of the poem. The human condition is one of privation; god grants the happiest of men no more than partial happiness. As the gods torment us, they also mock us with their own careless bliss. Man must be modest and enduring or even this partial hapiness will be taken from him. Yet just as the gods inflict on man pain and death, so also they have granted man the gift of finitude. Just as happiness is always partial, so also pain must come to some conclusion. The gods destroy, but at the last they bury their victims and there is an ending.

In the ceremonial context of the ransoming, Achilles is able, for the first time, to reflect upon himself and his own fate as one instance of a universal pattern. At this point Achilles, who throughout the poem has been bombarded by the moralisms of others, becomes himself a moralist. His moralism is no different from that already vainly recommended to him by Nestor, Phoenix, Apollo—that men should be *streptoi* and *tlētoi,* flexible and enduring. Their voices could not enter the situation in which Achilles so long was trapped; not even the gods could resolve his dilemma from the outside. But he can resolve it himself in a moment, once the context is no longer one of particular injuries and honors but of universal categories and values.

Priam and Achilles are enemies; that is their social relation. When they enter, through ceremony, the divine sphere, that relation disappears. They confront each other as independent beings; they become to each other aesthetic objects:

> Then Dardanian Priam marveled at Achilles,
> His size and quality; he seemed like the gods;
> And at Dardanian Priam wondered Achilles,
> Seeing his excellent face and hearing his voice,
> And so they joyed as they looked upon each other.
> (bk. 24, ll. 629–33)

The ceremony enables Achilles to know his situation and no longer merely experience it. What was baffling in its immediacy becomes lucid at a distance. Achilles surveys and comprehends his world and himself. That is the purification of Achilles.

On the other hand, nothing has changed. Priam is still Achilles' enemy, and their reconciliation is the fragile product of a fabricated ceremonial context. Any outcry from Priam would rend the fabric, and then Achilles would kill him (bk. 24, ll. 568–70, 582–86). Nor is Achilles reconciled with his own community; his dealings with Priam are explicitly an act to be done in secret, an act which his community does not permit (bk. 24, ll. 650–55). The purification of Achilles does not heal him. But he does come to repose, to food and sleep.

Throughout the *Iliad,* meals mark the moments of repose and integration. Achilles' refusal to eat after the ceremony of book 19 marks his reconciliation there with Agamemnon as partly illusory. All the resources of culture had been mobilized by Odysseus, that master of procedure: the assembly, the giving of gifts, the taking of an oath. The public order, property, the invocation of divine sanctions—all had proved inefficacious. But at the end of his reconciliation with Priam, Achilles eats. This last ceremony is efficacious, but on another level: culture is overcome.

ART AS THE NEGATION OF CULTURE

Culture confers on life a meaning and at the same time divides men from one another. Men are located and separated by the bonds of kinship and property, by loyalties and obligation, by status, role, and citizenship. Yet mankind remains a unity, most simply and profoundly on the level of organic life. To be human is to be a member of a species and to share with others a specific fate. That fate is to die; this Priam and Achilles recognize in their shared mourning. But the fate of the species is also to live, and this they recognize in their shared meal. In the midst of death we are in life. The reconciliation takes place on the level of nature, outside the human world; it is a ceremony founded on a universal concept of man qua man.

Since life takes on meaning only when formed by culture, this ceremony of reconciliation is not a discovery of meaning. It is rather an accurate recognition of meaninglessness. Achilles is not changed; his anger and his isolation remain. He is left, like Niobe, "consuming his sorrows." But the body of Hector is released and the poetic action is concluded.

The end of the *Iliad* echoes its beginning. In the beginning a father is refused the ransoming of his child; at the end a ransoming is permitted. In the beginning Achilles quarrels with a king; at the end he is reconciled with a king. Since the persons are different, however, these echoes are purely formal. The *Iliad* comes to a conclusion, not because the action imitated reaches a resolution, but because the poet has conferred on the event, in the manner of his telling it, a form and an ending.

We must distinguish the form of an action from its resolution. An action is resolved when the needs and demands of the actors are either met or crushed out. Such an outcome is *for the actors* and concludes the action on the ethical level. Form, on the other hand, is *for us*; an action is formed when it reveals a lucid meaning to the contemplative eye of the poet and his audience. The completion of its form concludes the action on the aesthetic level. This shift of levels is the work of imitation, which reduces experience and presents to us the problematic of life in a simplified, comprehensible form. The work of the imitative artist, as it is the invention of form, is also the discovery of meaning; but the meaning which art discovers in life is only theoretical, not practical. Through the work of art we comprehend in some way the order of things, but this comprehension does not necessarily give us a new basis for self-conscious action. Dramatic art rises from the dilemmas and contradictions of life, but it makes no promise to resolve these dilemmas; on the contrary, tragic art may well reach its highest formal perfection at the moment when it reveals to use these dilemmas as universal, pervasive, and necessary.

In Homeric language we would say that poetry is the work of *noos,* not *thumos.* The poet is detached; he recognizes. He stands apart from action and discerns its form. Contradiction, which baffles action and appears to the actor as formlessness, becomes (for the poet) itself a kind of form. The lucidity of a situation is often revealed at the moment we see it as held together by the tension of self-contradictory oppositions. In this sense the poet will discern form at the moment he ceases to see the situation as unresolved and comes to see it as unresolvable.

Thus, as culture is the purification of nature, so art is the purification of culture. That which baffles ethical forming, when further formed through imitative art, becomes itself a source of aesthetic form. As the forming of art is a further forming of forms already present in nature and culture, so it follows that artistic form is inclusive of culture and nature. Art may achieve form at the moment it recovers nature in relation to culture, recovers a comprehension of the intractability of nature to cultural form. In this sense art is the opposite of culture and at the same time completes culture. Poetry is about life and at the same time is a release from life. Through poetry man sees himself from a distance; poetry offers him not gratification but intelligibility. In tragic art, the pains and terrors of life are transformed from experiences to objects of knowledge; tragic art attains to form when it makes a lucid theoretical statement of the practical opacities of the human condition. In this sense tragic form is a "purification of these experiences."

It is a peculiarity of the epic that its heroes can, at certain moments, share the perspective of poet and audience and look down upon themselves. We observe such a shift of perspective in the occasions when the characters speak of their fate, that is, speak of their place in the story as a whole. In this respect, as in others, Achilles tests the limits of the heroic; when he commits himself to the killing of Hector, he sees his own death also before him and accepts it. He is thus an actor who both acts and knows his own actions as part of an unfolding pattern. He can do this because he is between man and god.

Specific to Homeric epic—and its descendant, Attic tragedy—are the Olympian gods, who, as we saw, are both part of the action and detached from it. They thus mediate between the actors and the audience. The gods' knowledge of fate is partial; otherwise they could not participate in the action. Their knowledge of fate is greater than men's; that is the mark of their greater detachment. They can intervene in the action on behalf of their favorites and to punish their enemies, but that intervention is, as we saw in the cases of Sarpedon and Hector, limited by the overriding necessities of the plot. The gods must allow the action to occur.

But then, after an action is completed, they can intervene to conclude it. This is intervention in quite a different sense. The gods have a concern for purity, that is, for the proper endings of things, a concern represented in their concern for funerals. They contrive the funeral of Sarpedon, protect the body of Patroclus, protect the body and contrive the funeral of Hector. Here the intervention is, as it were, from outside the action. The gods, who are outside any human community, can intervene to confer that purity which is beyond the power of human community; they can impose a limit on the impurity of combat. But this limitation, since it is from the outside, has an arbitrary element; it is less like the purity which rises from the orderings of culture and more like the purity imposed by the forming power of art.

Achilles, the hero who is closest to the gods, is at the end of the *Iliad* privileged to stand aside from his world and describe it. The ransoming of Hector is imposed upon him by Zeus; he accepts it because he shares to a degree the understanding of Zeus. He can look upon man as an ephemeral thing in nature and recognize him as unworthy of his hatred. Or, we must add, of his love.

The ransoming of Hector, by this reading, dissolves the distinction between victor and vanquished. Both are seen as sharing a common nature and a common fate. This is not to resolve the contradiction of combat but to erase it; for if the vanquished is no different from the victor, combat is meaningless. And if combat is meaningless, then community, for the sake of which combat is waged, is also meaningless.

Such a conclusion is not tolerable in life, for life must be lived in and for communities. That Achilles retains—with one part of his divided self—a place in the human world is marked by the anger which, he knows, at any moment might recover its power over him, which is only for a moment set aside by his contemplation of himself. In this contemplation Achilles—the only character in the *Iliad* who is himself a poet—shares the understanding of the poet. We thus leave him in a strange divided state, tensely poised between life and art. It is a strange paradox that conclusions which in life lead only to paralysis and despair in art are ennobling and sublime. That is the paradox of the tragic consciousness.

The ransoming of Hector is in contrast to the funeral games of Patroclus; the two stand to each other as drama to ceremony. In the games the reality of combat is concealed and denied; combat is transferred to a sphere in which it can be seen as unreal. This is an imitation which moves from reality to unreality.

In the ransoming of Hector the parties to conflict are also transferred— not to a different cultural sphere, but to a location outside culture. The distant inclusive perspective of the Olympian gods (which was at the first an invention of poets) becomes an Archimedean point where the poet, his audience, and even his hero can stand aside from the human world and judge it. The ransoming of Hector is a ceremony contrived by the god on behalf of the poet to complete and purify the poetic action. The ceremony of book 24 takes place outside the human world because the contradictions which it reveals cannot be resolved within the human world. The vision of man revealed in Achilles' two speeches is not a vision tolerable in practice. It is possible only in theory, in the moments when men like Glaucus, Sarpedon, and Achilles stand aside from the heroic role and see it. At such moments the hero is his own poet; the vision which he captures is proper to art. At these moments he abandons much of life—its particularities, affections, hopes—but something is gained. Art is an imitation which moves from reality to another reality—reduced, less rich in matter, but more coherent in form.

The action of the *Iliad* is an enactment of the contradictions of the warrior's role. The warrior on behalf of culture must leave culture and enter nature. In asserting the order of culture, he must deny himself a place in that order. That others may be pure, he must become impure.

Achilles and Hector experience the resulting tension differently. Hector's responsibilities outrun his powers. As he turns himself over to the sphere of nature, he loses reflective control and becomes subject to error. Error shames him before his community and separates him; he is the victim of the contradictory demands his community makes on him. The social order retains its meaning for him, but he can no longer find his place in it. And thus he dies.

Achilles retains his power but loses the social context which gave power responsible meaning. Achilles also is a victim of error—not primarily his own, but Agamemnon's. Wrong is done to him, and he is baffled. He feels his community shamed in relation to himself; the Greeks in their acquiescence to Agamemnon's injustice have become *outidanoi,* "mere nothings" (bk. 1, l. 231), and he himself would become *outidanos* if he were to consent (bk. 1, l. 293). Whereas Hector, in service to his community, loses his sense of identity and dissolves into fantasy and panic, Achilles, in order to save his identity, is forced to withdraw from his community—even in his return to action. Whereas Hector can do nothing but die, Achilles can do nothing but kill—kill, and despoil, torment others and himself. At the end of the poem he is tied to this fate still, and he knows it will lead to the destruction of Troy and to his own futile death.

The inner unity of the *Iliad* thus lies in the mirror opposition of the two heroes. In the concluding ceremony they are revealed to us—and to the surviving hero—as contrasting emblems of a single pattern. Achilles and

Hector represent the two aspects of war, aggressive and defensive, something suffered and something done. What is necessary and yet unjustifiable in fact justifies itself, at the end, as an object of poetic knowledge. What is incomprehensible in experience becomes patterned and even beautiful in the imitation of experience. And since poetic imitation, which claims to stand outside experience, is itself a human achievement, poetry claims for itself a place both outside and within the human world as it recovers for man a tragic meaning in the experience of meaninglessness.

> Zeus sent this evil portion, so that later,
> For men to come, we should be themes for song.
> (bk. 6, ll. 357–58)

Some Elements
of the Homeric Fantasy

Eric A. Havelock

The spell of the antique is strong in both epics, pervasively so in the associations surrounding proper names and epithets carried by some of the principal actors. Though the situations related in the stories belong to early Hellenism, the Hellenes are always archaized as Achaeans, Argives, or Danaans, a nomenclature not applicable (in this reference) in the historical period. Achilles, Ajax, Idomeneus, Hector (as well as some less conspicuous examples) have been doubtfully identified in the Linear B tablets, and the personality of Agamemnon still more doubtfully in the Hittite records. Odysseus, by contrast, may be a name without a pedigree. Mycenae "rich in gold" was in historical times a village, and Troy an uninhabited site.

ADVERSARY RELATIONSHIPS

Format no less than nomenclature shows the effect of traditional influence insofar as the ways in which the plots of both epics are constructed reflect the rules required for ease of memorization, rather than those required by a desire to record facts of contemporary history.

When Odysseus landed on his native soil to explore the reception he might meet with, he had already been accepted by the Phaeacians on their island utopia. If realism prevails in the harsh conditions on Ithaca, it is romanticism which had colored his reception in Phaeacia. Arriving at the palace of the king, the suppliant is graciously raised from the hearth, prom-

From *The Greek Concept of Justice: From Its Shadow in Homer to Its Substance in Plato.*
© 1978 by Eric A. Havelock. Harvard University Press, 1978.

ised a convoy on the morrow which will take him home, and is presented
by his host to an assembly, his guise transfigured by Athene's miraculous
power. The order is given to equip a ship for him. He is then conducted in
the company of the leading men of the city to a formal banquet for which
the king has been careful to provide appropriate entertainment. The bard
Demodocus receives a ceremonial summons to attend the banquet and re-
cites a lay:

> The muse aroused the singer to sing the fames of men—
> a song whose fame then reached to wide heaven—
> the strife [neikos] of Odysseus and Achilles—
> how on a time they contended [dērisanto] in luxuriant banquet
>   of the gods
> with terrifying utterances. The king of men, Agamemnon,
> rejoiced in his heart when the best of the Achaeans were
>   in contention [dērioonto]
>
> . . . .
>
> It was then that the beginning of woe toppled over
> for Trojans and Danaans because of the counsels of Zeus.
>
> (Odyssey, bk. 8, ll. 73–78, 81–82)

This saga, otherwise unrecorded except by commentators on the passage, sounds like an alternative version of the *Iliad*. Its theme is an angry
confrontation between two powerful men in the Greek army the result of
which brings an avalanche of trouble upon both Trojans and Achaeans, this
being in accordance with some decisions made by Zeus himself. These
terms are identical with those set forth in the preface to the *Iliad*, with the
difference that Odysseus is substituted for Agamemnon as the opponent of
Achilles.

Both versions illustrate what seems to be one of the laws controlling
the composition of mythos for oral commemoration. The action has to take
the form of confrontation between two or more parties. It is stories of
confrontation and struggle which are most seductive to the memory and
which give most pleasure in recall. War is a subject preferred to peace. This
meets one of the theoretic requirements of memorized speech, which likes
to follow not only metrical but thematic rhythms, taking their most obvious form in a pairing arrangement between two contending parties. Agents
who have to dominate the action are placed in adversary relationships. The
Greek terms are *neikos* and *eris*. The tale best remembered is the tale of duel.
The characters become wrestlers, battlers, fighters—*agonistae* (this term,
however, is post-Homeric). The competitive element in Greek culture has

recently attracted scholarly attention; I suggest here that in an orally managed culture the verbal record of what is going on is likely in any case to be created around competitive antagonisms between the personalities who are required as actors. The character of the record is governed in this respect by mnemonic considerations.

This principle of composition is characteristic of all epic as a genre. Its traces recur. The most natural way to incorporate confrontation at the center of narrative is to arrange the story within the context of the waging of war. A great war partly recollected and partly invented in oral epic becomes the necessary vehicle to serve as a repository for the storage of cultural information of the people whose exploits are sung in this way. This is not to say that such oral storage does not respond to certain realities in human history. Most language groups that have won for themselves cultural identities have done so in part by fighting their neighbors. But the point to bear in mind is that the compulsion to sing what is memorizable inevitably tends to compose history as though it consisted almost exclusively of military history. Such epics build themselves in response to the need to store and repeat and remember information. But that information covering the ethos and the nomos of ordinary daily life remains buried in the military context, so that the historical consciousness of the language group concerned becomes somewhat distorted. It is probably true that war as a way of life after the fashion of the *Iliad* has been a concept in part foisted upon Western culture by the mnemonic requirements of oral epic.

What is here being proposed is a functional, technical explanation of that poetry which we style "heroic." Its existence is usually explained in terms of the human consciousness, the supposed ideals of the people for whom such poetry was sung, and the same explanation is responsible for our imagining a society of warrior-aristocrats for whom such poetry was composed, whether in Greece or elsewhere. This is close to romantic nonsense. No society at any stage of the development of human civilization could ever have lived continuously as the Homeric so-called heroes are represented as living in the *Iliad*. In fact, as we have seen, below the level of the military narrative the outline of a perfectly normative society, political and familial, becomes evident. The Trojan War itself is a narrative fantasy designed to evoke sympathetic response from a culture which was all too familiar with wars but never on such a total scale or with such concentration.

Action arranged as confrontation serving as a principle of composition can take a second form, that of the dangerous journey in which an individual or family are pitted against both natural and human enemies through which they thread their way toward a satisfactory terminus which is supposed to be a return home. It is relevant to observe that the original Hebrew epics which lie behind the biblical narrative of events up to the beginning of David's reign combine these two principles of composition: first, the journeys of the patriarchs in search of homes new and old; then the journey of the Israelites to seek a new home; then the "Wars of Jehovah," still traceable in the books of Joshua and Judges, supposedly waged with the aim of occupying Canaan, but represented as a final homecoming to a land long promised—in short, a Hebrew *Odyssey,* or several *Odysseys,* followed by a Hebrew *Iliad.* Hazardous journeys conceived on a grand scale are, like wars, part of the storyteller's stock in trade, and for the same reason. They are memorizable. Both types provide an overall context, a kind of portmanteau of memory, within which cultural data can be contained and recollected as the remembered rhythm travels the same road over again.

The Trojan War and the *nostos* of Odysseus, respectively, are therefore fantasies which serve as excuse for the presence of nonfantastic elements. They carry the hallmarks of fantasy, one of which is exaggeration of dimension. The war is a ten-year war, the journey home is a ten-year journey. The war pits a host of warriors assembled from the entire Achaean world against a city which we are encouraged to imagine is not just any city but an imperial capital wealthy and populous. The fighting is carefully structured in a series of duels and confrontations capped by an inspired and miraculous onslaught on the part of a single man who is supposed to take on the forces of Nature herself as his antagonists. The war even invades heaven, dividing the deities into warring camps.

The equally fantastic journey is so designed that in the course of confronting alien hazards, hostile men and creatures, storm, hunger, and shipwreck, the protagonist alone survives through a combination of superhuman skill, prudence, and daring. His total isolation is then pitted against a group of enemies numbering over a hundred. He reveals himself to them with some advantage of surprise, and the fantastic encounter has the improbable result that he kills them all together. The mythos has to make some concession to the probabilities by supplying him with one divine and three human assistants of inferior age and rank.

Kings and Queens

If the remembered mythos requires to be cast in the form of a narrative of acts by living agents, and if the cultural function of such narrative is enhanced by historical fantasy, the agents concerned must inevitably show some tendency to enjoy an enlarged status and inflated importance. In the context of military confrontation they become generals, commanders of great masses of men; in their civil aspect they become kings and queens and princes and princesses, grandiose versions of members of that public for whose benefit the oral epic is being composed. It is in any case very difficult to describe the confusions of actual conflict coherently except in terms of the leadership, as readers of *War and Peace* are well aware.

Agamemnon in his civil aspect becomes a monarch "who holds power over all Argives and the Achaeans obey him" (bk. 1, ll. 78–79). This is fantasy. The extent of his actual authority and status, as revealed in the course of the story, is a very different affair. His opposite number in civil life is Priam with his consort Hecuba, an absolute monarch of an empire vaguely defined and never operative in the actual plot. There is less fantasy in the portrait of Odysseus in the *Odyssey,* mainly because the plot requires his humble disguise, but he is not infrequently identified as the monarch ruling over Ithaca in its entirety, a status directly at variance with the existence of all the magnates who want to marry his putative widow. More obviously, the polity of the Phaeacians, though exhibiting a lifestyle which is obviously a utopian version of that current in the Hellenic maritime polis, is represented as enjoying the rule of a beneficent monarchy exercised by an idealized king and queen.

The commingling of romanticism and realism can be appreciated by analyzing the way in which this king summons an agora at the beginning of the eighth book of the *Odyssey* to deal with the problem of the mysterious visitor in their midst. The poet makes clear that it is indeed an agora (bk. 8, ll. 5 and 12), but because of the monarchical setting the council of elders is summoned by the king first. They are in effect represented as his courtiers and accordingly take their seats (ll. 4–6). Only then is the herald dispatched to perform his function of going through the city to summon the meeting. He addresses "each man," but the object of his address is then described as "leaders and counsellors of the Phaeacians" (l. 11). The agora fills up, and then the stone seats are again occupied, this time in the proper order (l. 16), implying the presence of two different bodies, one consisting of the standing citizens, the other the seated council. But no deliberation follows. The king stands up, harangues and gives orders, and leads his princes in a kind of ceremonial exit to escort the stranger to the palace for a banquet. There is no mention of the termination of the agora; its existence has been forgotten.

EXAGGERATION OF DIMENSION

The inflation of rank and station required by fantasy finds its counter-part in the exaggeration, already noted, of numbers and quantities, a per-

sistent trait observable in all oral epic. Priam is equipped with fifty married
sons who require fifty bedrooms plus apparently twelve daughters and
sons-in-law with twelve bedrooms (bk. 24, ll. 41–50). Apparently, by the
time Priam confronts Achilles they have all been wiped out (bk. 24, l. 494),
though earlier in the narrative the poet seems to allow for survivors (l. 260).
The household of Odysseus requires the services of fifty maid servants
(*Odyssey*, bk. 22, l. 421; so also Alcinous, *Odyssey*, bk. 7, l. 603); the com-
petitors for Penelope's hand number 108 plus eight servitors, one herald,
and one bard (*Odyssey*, bk. 16, ll. 247–51). How, we may ask, could the
estate of Odysseus, even imagining him to be monarch of all Ithaca, accommodate these numbers not for a single year but for a ten-year orgy? No
wonder that the dimensions of his megaron have to be extended to accommodate such a horde. In fact, they are presented as a muster of leading men
drawn from Ithaca and the adjacent islands and mainland. The poet supplies
a catalogue of their kingdoms. All this is complete fantasy.

Equal exaggeration is extended to the material resources employed by
this society. The meals eaten in the *Iliad* and the *Odyssey* are gargantuan.
The gifts proffered by Agamemnon to Achilles as part of the reconciliation
are perhaps conceivable as worthy of an oriental monarchy, but they would
bankrupt any Greek state. Apparently, a large part of them is supposed to
be in storage on Trojan soil during the campaign, loot accumulated and
guarded during nine years of fighting (bk. 9, ll. 122–48, with ll. 149–56, a
supplementary list of towns; at bk. 19, l. 238 a retinue is needed to produce
them). The gifts heaped upon Odysseus by the Phaeacians are less imperial
(no women are included) but equally extravagant (*Odyssey*, bk. 8, ll. 392–
94, 403–5, 424–28, 438–42; *Odyssey*, bk. 13, ll. 10–19, 213–19 [an additional
levy], 363–70). These lists in the *Iliad* and the *Odyssey* are repetitive and
obsessive; the narratives make a point of stressing that the objects are to be
counted (bk. 9, l. 121) and placed on display (bk. 19, ll. 172 and 189;
Odyssey, bk. 8, l. 424), to be looked at as at a modern wedding ceremony.
The magic vessel which transports Odysseus to his home transports also his
hoard, which on arrival has to be carefully stowed away in hiding by
Athene's instructions (*Odyssey*, bk. 13, ll. 363–71). The epics glory in conspicuous consumption. Such descriptions reinforce the spell over the memory of the listeners. A culture in reality based on meager economic resources
and a simple lifestyle will respond to their fascination with a kind of vicarious greed. Readers of the Count of Monte Cristo will recognize a modern
Odysseus, not merely by his early persecution, his adventures, and his
disguise, but by that rich and mysterious hoard of treasure which his adventures gained for him.

These examples of romantic dimension are not very subtle; they could be multiplied with ease. Fantasy, however, can also intrude at a level which could be described as purely verbal and which may elude notice because its effects are unconscious. Inherently, it is achieved by the fact that so much of Homer's vocabulary operates on two levels, in the sense that given words can describe relationships or acts which are either Mycenaean in the fantasy sense or Hellenic in the contemporary and realistic sense. Four such can serve as typical examples of this verbal behavior: the Greek words *basileus*, *heros*, *skeptron*, and *megaron*.

The Title *Basileus*

The reader of Homer does not need to be reminded how frequently the poet employs the word *basileus*, which is commonly translated to mean a "king." This coloration derives from its association as a title with three men: Agamemnon and Priam in the *Iliad* and Alcinous in the *Odyssey*. Its appearance in the contexts controlled by these personalities is rather infrequent. But all three of them in the epic mythoi are represented as enjoying a status which is unique and royal, equivalent to our monarch or sole ruler, occupying palaces, and ruling over empires, in the case of Agamemnon and Priam, or over a city and people, in the case of Alcinous. In these contexts, it is implied that their rule is autocratic.

Basileus is employed to identify Agamemnon in the opening lines of the *Iliad*: a plague had descended on the army because "Apollo was angry with the king." More explicitly, after Achilles has quarreled with Agamemnon, Nestor admonishes him in the following terms:

> Do not contend or strive in confrontation with a king,
> seeing that never is the portion of honor like to that
>   of other men
> which is assigned to a scepter-holding king to whom Zeus
>   has given glory;
> you may be the stronger because of your divine birth,
> but he is superior for he rules as lord over more people.
>
> (bk. 1, ll. 277–81)

The position of Agamemnon is unique precisely because of the extent of his authority. He is a monarch, Achilles is not. The word which describes his exercise of power is *anassein*; the correlative noun is *anax* which recurs in the formula "Agamemnon, lord-king of men." *Basileus*, therefore, in this context is treated as the equivalent of *anax*.

The poet takes occasion to underline the same status of Agamemnon as he describes the military review which occupies book 2:

> Lord-king Agamemnon stood up,
> holding the scepter that Hephaestos had wrought.
>
> . . . .
>
> Thyestes left it to Agamemnon to wield
> to rule as lord-king over many islands and Argos.
> He leaned on it and addressed the Argives.
>
> (bk. 2, ll. 100–101, 107–9)

Though the title *basileus* is not used, this is fortuitous. The verb once more is *anassein*, to exercise the power of an *anax*, a monarch.

Again in book 9, as Nestor tactfully opens up the subject of a possible conciliatory move on Agamemnon's part toward Achilles, he ceremoniously addresses him:

> Son of Atreus renowned, lord-king [*anax*] of men Agamemnon,
> in you I shall cease, with you I begin, for that over many
> peoples you are lord-king [*anax*] and Zeus has put
> into your hands
> scepter and formularies that you may administer counsel
> to them.
>
> (bk. 9, ll. 96–99)

Once more the particular title *basileus* does not occur, but we infer from correlation between this and other passages that in the case of Agamemnon *basileus* is equivalent to *anax*, itself a Mycenaean title.

The same rule seems to be followed for Priam, who carries the title *anax*. It is only in the conclusion of the epic that Achilles takes occasion to note the extent of Priam's empire (bk. 24, ll. 543ff.), whereupon the poet calls him "*basileus*" (bk. 24, l. 680) and finally "god-nurtured *basileus*" in the last line but one of the poem. Throughout the *Iliad* his name recurs formulaically in the role of paterfamilias; at the realistic level of the concluding episodes he becomes simply an aged man, with corresponding titles.

In the seventh book of the *Odyssey* Alcinous likewise occupies a large and luxurious palace and apparently rules authoritatively over his people. The title *basileus* is attached to him with some regularity (*Odyssey*, bk. 7, ll. 46, 55, 141, etc.).

The same title in the same monarchical sense is occasionally linked associatively with Odysseus. Mentor, reproaching the agora of Ithaca for their indifference to the memory of Odysseus, exclaims

> No need for any man to be of ready kindness and gentle,
> even a scepter-bearing *basileus*
> . . . .
> since no man now remembers Odysseus
> or the people whom he ruled as lord-king [*anassein*]
> and as a father was gentle to them.
> (bk. 2, ll. 230–31, 233–34)

The complaint is repeated in the same terms by Athene on Olympus, and when Odysseus disguised first greets Penelope, he compares her ceremoniously to

> a blameless *basileus* who god-fearing
> among many men and mighty ruling-as-lord [*anassōn*]
> sustains justices-that-are-good.
> (bk. 19, ll. 109–11)

It is proper to isolate these examples of a term otherwise used with a different coloration, for the contexts recall the conditions of monarchy as it was exercised among the Mycenaeans. The coloration is prehistoric and constitutes a forceful element in the fantasy, suggesting that the leading personalities of the poems were themselves prehistoric and therefore that the society described is also prehistoric and monarchical.

The fantasy was continued in the plots of Athenian drama produced during the fifth century. These for the most part mirror the preoccupations of contemporary society, which, however, are transferred into the lives of kings and queens, reigning prehistorically for the most part in such centers as Thebes, Athens, Argos, and Sparta. Such monarchies at the time when the plays were offered for performance were antiquarian curiosities. But the dramatic action acquired obvious advantages when it focused on the lives of a few powerful people, men and women. It became at once intensified and simplified. The *basileis* and *anaktes,* the kings and lords who thus reappear in the post-Homeric era, induce the modern reader of Homer to accept with some readiness the proposition that Homer's world was likewise a monarchical world. So indeed it was felt to be by its audiences insofar as they submitted readily enough to the required fantasy. But equally they were aware of a second level at which the society of Homer operated within contemporary concerns, the level of the city-state.

This can be appreciated by noticing the second level at which the term *basileus* is used, one which would correspond to its original meaning in the prehistoric period, if the decipherment of Linear B tablets is to be trusted. It has been discovered in them and has been translated as "feudal lord" or as "mayor," being taken to identify local officials of towns subordinate to Knossos and Pylos, and under the authority of the kings who lived there. In Homer it is more often pluralized than used in the singular of a monarch. All the leading characters of the *Iliad* can be styled *basileus,* and from time to time they constitute a committee of *basileis* which functions as a kind of council of war. The city-state ruled by Alcinous in the *Odyssey,* it turns out, contains twelve *basileis* besides Alcinous himself. Antinous, leading spirit among the suitors of Penelope, is styled *basileus* (bk. 24, l. 179). The question arises: Can these really be "kings"? Does the translation not convey a misleading suggestion? Should they even be equated with "princes"? Princes after all are members of royal courts. Is not the whole concept of royalty inapplicable to societies in which these pluralized *basileis* lived? By following the logic of its pluralization, *basileus* can be used as an adjective—a *basileus*-man—and even more surprisingly, the adjective can be compared in degree: a man can be "more of a *basileus*" than another. The inference is that *basileus* at this level of meaning indicates any person of importance, and importance can be a matter of degree. The term, in short, should be equated with many others in Homer which equally indicate people we would call "magnates," "leading men," and the like: "O leaders and magistrates" was a favorite form of address— *hēgētores* and *medontes.* At other times we hear of the *stratēgos* and the *kosmētōr,* the "army leader" and the "organizer"; of the *archos,* or "ship's captain"; the *dunamenos,* or "man of power"; the *aristos,* "the top man" (applied to the suitor who will win Penelope, *Odyssey,* bk. 16, l. 76); the *koiranos,* the "authority." All these terms can be pluralized. The suitors of Penelope are described in the following terms:

> All who have power over the islands being top men [*aristoi*]
> and all who have authority [*koiraneousi*] through craggy Ithaca.

The formula is repeated by Eumaeus and by Penelope (*Odyssey,* bk. 16, l. 122 and *Odyssey,* bk. 19, l. 130).

I noted above the extraordinary number of these suitors. These are not royal personages or monarchs; they are gentlemen, country squires, local potentates in their communities. The verbs which express their exercise of power are really applicable to the exercise of what we would call "influence." But it is equally true that the same words at the level of fantasy can recall the autocracies of Mycenae. The problematic status of Telemachus, an issue central to the developing story, is debated early in the epic (*Odyssey,* bk. 1, ll. 383–409), in terms which illustrate the fluid confusion of archaic and contemporary within the same vocabulary: (1) Ithaca is ruled by a hereditary monarch (ll. 386–87); (2) the monarchy is not hereditary (ll. 400–401); (3) there is no monarchy, but a large number of local authorities (ll. 393–94); (4) winning such authority is prized for the prestige and money it brings (ll. 391–93); (5) "lord-king" (*anax*) is the title of a man of property (ll. 397–98).

At the realistic level the "aristocracies," so called, of Homer are small-town elites, not formally defined by birth or inheritance, though inheritance can become an issue, as in the *Odyssey*. Status depends on money and wealth more than on military effectiveness. But because of the double reference, on the one hand to prehistoric kingdoms half-remembered, on the other to contemporary city-state conditions in which the leading men run things as leading men always do, the citizens who listened to these sagas could feel a confused identification of themselves as the demos and *laos* who lived in the city-state, or as members of a real class of influential families whose decisions could guide the city provided they were approved in the agora, or finally as kings and princes living in Mycenaean palaces with hordes of mythical retainers.

In this guise they thought themselves to be the heirs of Homer living the life of true Greeks on the heroic scale insofar as an aspiration to emulate past ways was instilled by a recital of the epics. This is the secret of those "ideals" which historians have ascribed to the Greeks without knowing quite where they came from, or indeed what they were. The fantasy was essential for this purpose. It supplied not merely cultural identification for the Hellenes of the historic era but an intensified consciousness, so that they were capable of living in two worlds at once.

A fantasy which was functional for the Hellenes has become an intellectual trap for moderns, creating the presumption that Homeric society was one of "tribal kingship," supposedly intermediate between Mycenae and the city-state of historical times. There is no hard evidence that such a polity in such a period ever existed. The portrait of Alcinous and his court and his master-mariners in the seventh book of the *Odyssey* has been superimposed upon a lifestyle which, as previously indicated, is that of a Greek maritime colony. To be sure, his court has many parallels with the so-called courts established by those individuals who from time to time exercised authority in the Greek city-states in the early Hellenic period, and who are styled "tyrants," which is a transliteration but also in effect a mistranslation of the Greek *tyrannos*. The tyrants were popular leaders, usually acclaimed by the agoras of their respective cities, vested with powers which, though short-lived, were to prove beneficial to the demos, and generous in their patronage of poets and musicians. Their era would coincide with the last period of oral composition, when the epics were achieving their final form, and it cannot be excluded that behind the portrait of Alcinous there is concealed the gratitude of a bard to his patron.

THE "SCEPTER"

The *basileus* in his monarchical aspect carries a *skēptron,* but not the scepter of medieval and Renaissance usage when the availability of a literate bureaucracy had rendered the scepter ceremonial. In Homer it is a club or staff held in the hands as a symbol of oral authority—the right to speak—as opposed to the duty to listen. This symbol of a common object is also used ambivalently. It refers to a procedure carried out in two different modes. In a passage of the second book of the *Iliad* already noted Agamemnon's monarchical authority is given a legitimacy conveyed by the fact that his scepter had descended to him ultimately from the gods. Similarly, Nestor's tactful admonition to Agamemnon in book 9 recalls the fact that "scepter and formularies are placed by Zeus in your hands." In this sense the scepter is behaving prehistorically. We might say that its possession is a monopoly of the Mycenaean throne. But at the beginning of the *Iliad,* as the quarrel opens between Achilles and Agamemnon, Achilles is holding a scepter which he dashes on the ground, exclaiming

> Now indeed do the sons of the Achaeans
> wield it in their hands, even the managers-of-rights,
>   who the formularies
> do conserve under Zeus.

This would seem to describe the scepter as representing an authority vested not in any monarch but in a body of magistrates, specialists who had the duty to preserve the "dooms" which in book 9 are supposed to be solely in the hands of the monarch. It is tempting to infer that in book 9 Nestor is commemorating the prehistoric practice which allowed the king to hold in his hand the tablets of the law inscribed in Linear B, whereas Achilles in book 1 commemorates the guarding of the law in historical times through oral memorization entrusted to officials especially trained for this task. This is consistent with the import of a scene described as embossed upon Achilles' shield which describes a litigation between two parties in purely oral terms. Such would be the necessary practice in the city-state of early Hellenism; and the combination of two such different memories in a single epic, though inconsistent in themselves, would accord with the mingling of fantasy and reality necessary to the epic's function as a cultural encyclopedia.

THE MEGARON

One of the commonest nouns in the diction of Homer and of Greek tragedy is *megaron,* a hall, or the plural *megara,* halls. The "megaron type" has become a technical term in architectural history inspired by the palace plans uncovered at Mycenae and Pylos from which the Greek temple plan is viewed as derivative. Accordingly, elaborate attempts have been made to identify Homer's description of a megaron, particularly the megaron of Odysseus, with the prehistoric model. Such labor is misapplied. In its Mycenaean aspect the megaron is supposed to be fronted by an *aulē,* a court, with colonnades (*aithousai*) and perhaps a forecourt, porticoes, and gateways. However, we have already viewed the suitors for Penelope's hand sitting in front of Odysseus's house on hides spread over the dung-laden farmyard. In more grandiose settings Zeus in the *Iliad* not infrequently assembles his family council in a complex which is recognizably Mycenaean. If prehistoric memories play much part in the politics of the *Iliad,* the place to look for them is in the councils held on Olympus. Zeus for the most part is a true monarch, a Mycenaean autocrat, though there is a powerful consort by his side, and both of them sit on thrones. His court is strictly limited in numbers, a *boule* without an agora; it consists of blood relatives, including females, who are equal in rank to the males. Meetings are held in Zeus's house (bk. 20, l. 10, bk. 15, l. 85) in a kind of throne room, with perhaps an anteroom and a forecourt with a colonnade and seats (bk. 20, l. 11). It is this architectural complex which resembles what archaeologists describe as the "megaron of the classic Mycenaean type," though the descriptions are not wholly consistent. When the members of the court meet and are seated, there is a "session" (bk. 8, l. 439), but a session is equally an occasion for drinking (bk. 20, l. 101, bk. 15, ll. 86ff.) and for eating (bk. 15, l. 95), so that the throne room is in effect also a dining room, where if Zeus is absent Themis becomes the presiding deity (bk. 15, l. 95), perhaps because Hera has arrived late (bk. 15, l. 84), though it is significant that Themis, goddess of law, is elsewhere at the realistic level (*Odyssey,* bk. 2, l. 69) assigned the symbolic role of "seating and dismissing the agora," where law is administered. At the opening of book 20 the narrative describes Zeus in the role of a summoner of an agora, uniquely so. The mass audience is provided by the rivers, nymphs, and springs (bk. 20, l. 7ff). Nevertheless, they are somehow accommodated in the forecourt, a fact which allows Zeus to address them. There may be a blend here of fantasy and reality: the fantasy being the Mycenaean palace, the reality a civic agora surrounded by colonnades with a council house at one end. The fact is that the megaron continued to symbolize any dwelling of superior status, from a palace to a farmhouse. It remains a poetic word, a fantasy word. The personage who in Balfe's opera sings "I dreamt that I dwelt in marble halls" is certainly no character out of Homer, but the fantasy in which the building exists is Homeric all the same. The proportions of Odysseus's megaron would be required to accommodate over a hundred guests plus fifty maids plus more servitors unspecified; its dimension for poetic purposes have to be heroic, but only for poetic purposes.

The "Hero"

The illusion of a supposed "tribal kingship" is only part of a larger misconception about the society reported in Homer's poems, one that is summed up when we speak of the age of Homer as a "heroic age" and of his epics as "heroic poetry." No conception is more firmly rooted in the modern mind. Yet its existence is one more tribute to the power of Homer's fantasy to control our reading of his surviving text. The term "hero" in the sense in which we use it, the romanticized sense, is only rarely reflected in Homeric usage. Before Odysseus completes his account to Alcinous of his visit to Hades, his narrative pauses, and this allows the king to ask him,

> Did you see any of your godlike comrades who with you
> followed to Ilium together and there met their fate?
> (*Odyssey,* bk. 11, ll. 371–72)

Odysseus responds by adding a supplement, in which he recounts how he conversed with Agamemnon and Achilles, sought to converse with Ajax, viewed as in a spectacle Minos, Orion, Tityos, Tantalus, Sisyphus, and listened to converse from Heracles. The narrative device has the effect of placing this list of names in a special classification, in which three of the great dead of the Trojan War are included with mythical figures who may be regarded as pre-Trojan. The inference is encouraged that certain leading characters of the *Iliad* have been consigned by tradition to a category of supermen and were so accepted by the audience at epic recital. But they are such because, being dead and gone, they belong to a remote past. When Odysseus is about to leave Hades, he waits a moment:

> if perchance one might still come
> of the hero men who perished aforetime.
> (*Odyssey,* bk. 11, ll. 628–29)

When in the last book of the epic the ghosts of the slain suitors encounter company in Hades, they discover Achilles commiserating with Agamemnon:

Son of Atreus, we used to say that to Zeus the thunderer
you above all hero men were dear for all your days.
(*Odyssey*, bk. 24, ll. 24–25)

The formulaic expression "hero men" in both these instances is applied to
"ghosts," and the same is true of one usage of "hero" in the opening lines of
the *Iliad*, an unlucky place for it to occur, so far as Homeric interpretation is
concerned, for it can mislead the reader into supposing that "hero" is a title
routinely conferred upon all Greeks who fought at Troy. The wrath of
Achilles, we are told, was the agent which

did hurl to Hades many stalwart ghosts
of heroes, but made of the men [*autous*] takings for dogs
and all birds.
(bk. 1, ll. 3–5)

To speak of a "stalwart ghost" is for Homer a contradiction in terms, and
when the same formula is reused in the eleventh book (l. 55), the poet
prefers more logically to speak of "stalwart heads." The intention of his
introduction is to place the label "hero" summarily upon those stalwarts
who fought at Troy, but being now dead they have to become, rather
awkwardly, "stalwart ghosts." It is almost as though the notion of "heroes" as a class, described in the *Iliad* as falling at Troy, and now constitut-
ing a vanished generation, is taking shape in the poet's mind, and this is
borne out by another passage (bk. 12, l. 23) where it is recalled how by
Simois and Scamender "fell the race [*genos*] of godlike men." For the poet
himself, the characters of his *Iliad* are by now becoming legendary.

But otherwise, as applied to the living, the reference of hero is com-
monplace: particularly in the formula of address used, for example, by
Agamemnon in the episode in book 2 already noted where he has mustered
the army:

O Danaans, my dear heroes, servants of Ares.

This is simply a general's address to his army as "fellow soldiers." The so-
called heroes consist of all ranks, as is clear from another formula which
speaks of Athene's spear in the following terms:

wherewith she subdues the ranks of hero men,
even those with whom the daughter of the mighty sire
is angered.
(*Odyssey*, bk. 1, ll. 100–101)

It appears to describe under the guise of divine action what happens when troops break ranks in panic. Again, when Achilles summons an agora to witness his reconciliation, the general audience which is expected to attend (and which includes civilians) is twice described by the formula "hero-Achaeans."

Nor, as we might be tempted to think, does *hērōs* necessarily mean a fighting man. It can stand as an epithet of the bard, the herald, the craftsman, not to mention the Phaeacians, that peaceful society of master mariners. The two companions of Achilles who in the last scene with Priam have taken Patroclus's place and wait on Achilles (*therapontes*) and take orders from him along with the servants (bk. 24, ll. 590 and 643) are called "heroes" (ll. 474 and 573), but Achilles is not. In short, the hero was any stout fellow, whatever his status and function, as indicated by the pertinent entry in the earlier editions of Liddel and Scott's *Greek Lexicon*, "applied to any free man of the ante-Hellenic age," an observation regrettably omitted from the latest edition. It should be added that the epithet is frequently attached to the aged, somewhat like our "sire."

Since whole books have been and will continue to be written on such things as heroic poetry, Homer and heroism, Homer and the heroic tradition, and the like, it may be pertinent to add a footnote on the probable origins of the concept of the heroic as applied to a type of society and a genre of poetry. In post-Homeric Greek, a *hērōs* is someone dead, but bearing the reputation of important achievement in life, often in the role of supposed ancestor, such as the founder of a city, the "eponymous" of a tribe. Such "heroes" were frequently the object of local cults. This usage seems to have only tenuous connection with a presumed "heroic age" of Trojan warriors, the seeds of which appear to have been sown when Hesiod inserted in the myth of the Four Ages of Man a fifth, which he put in fourth place, consisting of those who fought at Troy, by which he means the characters in the Homeric poems. The intimacy of Hesiod's relationship to these poems will be explored [elsewhere]. Hesiod himself was canonized by the Greeks of the fifth and later centuries, and his "heroic age" was accepted by Aristotle as a formal historical category: "The leaders of the ancients alone were heroes: the people were just human beings." This view allows the philosopher to use the phrase "in the heroic times" as a chronological definition. From the Hellenistic age the concept passed to Rome, was accepted by Cicero and the Augustan poets, canonized by Horace, enshrined by Virgil's *Aeneid,* and passed in its Latinized version first to the Normans and then to the Renaissance. Milton is perfectly familiar with it:

Th'Heroic Race
That fought at Theb's and Ilium.

Applying the term deliberately to Samson, who

> heroicly hath finished
> A life heroic,

he enlarges it out of its Greek context and converts it into a general historical type. During the eighteenth and nineteenth centuries this late classical conception of the heroic was applied to early European societies and their sagas, so far as known. The tendency of Germans to romanticize their Teutonic and Nordic origins had a considerable effect upon German scholarship, nor should the widespread influence of Wagnerian opera be forgotten. English publicists like Carlyle could commit themselves to a whole view of human history summed up in such a title as *Heroes and Hero Worship*. Finally, the concept has been extended in the twentieth century to cover the surviving oral poetry of the Balkans and to the characters commemorated therein.

If the characters of the *Iliad* and *Odyssey* are "heroes" in any meaningful sense, it is only because they gave to the early Hellenes a sense of identity and of history rather larger than life size. But they could not have done this if they had been restricted to representing purely hypothetical personages living a lifestyle distinct from that of the Greek city-state.

The noun *kouros* (*kourētēs*), a "youth," "young man," "fellow," or "wight," has a coverage of meaning similar to that of *hērōs*, coextensive with the population portrayed. The warriors of the *Iliad* are *kouroi*, and so are those who wait on them (bk. 19, l. 248); so are the suitors in the *Odyssey* (bk. 17, l. 174), and also those who wait on them (*Odyssey*, bk. 1, l. 148); so are the peaceful seafarers who inhabit Alcinous' kingdom, so are the statues holding lamps which illuminate his banquet hall (*Odyssey*, bk. 8, ll. 35, 40, 48; bk. 7, l. 100), and so also the male inhabitants of Athens (bk. 2, l. 551). The term is worth mentioning, as an appendix to *hērōs*, if only because its usage in Homer faithfully corresponds to the wide dispersion of *kouroi* (not to mention *korai*) as funerary statues in the orientalizing and archaic periods of the Greek city-state. Homeric epic and Hellenic art alike report a concept of manhood (and womanhood) which . . . is coextensive with the citizenry of the Greek polis.

Poetic Visions of Immortality for the Hero

Gregory Nagy

Upon having their lifespan cut short by death, heroes receive as consolation the promise of immortality, but this state of immortality after death is located at the extremes of our universe, far removed from the realities of the here-and-now. We in this life have to keep reminding ourselves that the hero who died is still capable of pleasure, that he can still enjoy such real things as convivial feasts in the pleasant company of other youths like him. It is this sort of spirit that the *Banquet Song for Harmodios* is composed, honoring the young man who had achieved the status of being worshiped as a hero by the Athenians for having died a tyrant killer:

> Harmodios, most *phílos*! Surely you are not at all dead,
> but they say that you are on the Isles of the Blessed,
> the same place where swift-footed Achilles is,
> and they say that the worthy Diomedes, son of Tydeus,
>   is there too.

The perfect tense of the verb οὐ . . . τέθνηκας "you are not dead" leaves room for the reality of the hero's death: it is not that he did not die, but that he is not dead now. The fact of death, even for the hero, is painfully real and preoccupying. Consider this excerpt from a *thrênos* by Simonides:

> Not even those who were before, once upon a time,
> and who were born *hēmítheoi* as sons of the lord-gods,

From *The Best of the Achaeans: Concepts of the Hero in Archaic Greek Poetry.* © 1979 by the Johns Hopkins University Press.

not even they reached old age by bringing to a close a lifespan
that is without toil, that is *áphthitos* [unfailing], that is
without danger.

Not even heroes, then, have a *bíos* "lifespan" that is *áphthitos* "unfailing";
they too have to die before the immortality that is promised by the *thrênoi*
comes true.

Even in the *Aithiopis,* the immortality reached by Achilles is not an
immediate but a remote state: after death, the hero is permanently removed
from the here-and-now of the Achaeans who mourn him. For them, the
immediacy of Achilles after death has to take the form of a funeral, which
includes not only such things as the singing of *thrênoi* over his body but also—
even after Achilles has already been transported to his immortal state—the
actual building of a funeral mound and the holding of funeral games in his
honor. I conclude, then, that even in the *Aithiopis* the immortality of Achilles
is predicated on his death, which is the occasion for the *thrênoi* sung by the
Muses as a consolation for his death. In the *Iliad,* the theme of immortality is
similarly predicated on the death of Achilles, but here the focus of consolation
is not on the hero's afterlife, but rather, on the eternal survival of the epic that
glorifies him.

As we now proceed to examine the diction in which this theme is
expressed, we must keep in mind the words in the *thrênos* of Simonides:
even the heroes themselves fail to have a *bíos* "lifespan" that is *áphthitos*
"unfailing." In the *Iliad,* Achilles himself says that he will have no *kléos* if he
leaves Troy and goes home to live on into old age (bk. 9, ll. 414–16)—but
that he will indeed have a *kléos* that is *áphthiton* "unfailing" (bk. 9, l. 413) if
he stays to fight at Troy and dies young. The same theme of the eternity
achieved by the hero *within epic* recurs in Pindar's *Isthmian 8,* and again it is
expressed with the same root *phthi-* as in *áphthito-*; he will have a *kléos* that is
everlasting (cf. *Odyssey,* bk. 24, ll. 93–94):

> But when he [Achilles] died, the songs did not leave him,
> but the Heliconian Maidens [Muses] stood by his funeral pyre
>   and his funeral mound,
> and they poured forth a *thrênos* that is very renowned.
> And so the gods decided
> to hand over the worthy man, dead as he was [*phthímenos*],
>   to the songs of the goddesses [Muses].
>
> (Pindar I.8.62–66)

The key word of the moment, *phthí-menos,* which I translate here in the conventional mode as "dead," is formed from a root that also carries with it the inherited metaphorical force of vegetal imagery: *phthi-* inherits the meaning "wilt," as in *karpoû phthísin* "wilting of the crops" (Pindar *Paean* 9.14). Through the comparative method, we can recover kindred vegetal imagery in another derivative of the root, the epithet *á-phthi-ton* as it applies to the *kléos* of Achilles at book 9, line 413.

As in the *Iliad,* the contrast in this Pindaric passage concerns the mortality of Achilles and the immortality conferred by the songs of the Muses. More specifically, Pindar's words are also implying that the epic of Achilles amounts to an eternal outflow of the *thrênos* performed for Achilles by the Muses themselves. In this light, let us now consider again the Homeric evidence. In the *Odyssey,* the description of the funeral that the Achaeans hold for Achilles includes such details as the *thrênos* of the Muses (*Odyssey,* bk. 24, ll. 60–61) and ends with the retrospective thought that "in this way" (ὥς: 93) the hero kept his fame even after death and that he will have a *kléos* that is everlasting (ll. 93–94). We get more evidence from the *Iliad* in the form of a correlation between theme and form. The forms are the actual names of *Akhil(l)eús* (from *Akhí-lāụos "having a grieving *lāós"*) and *Patroklées* ("having the *kléos* of the ancestors"). As I have argued, the figure of *Patro-kléēs* is in the *Iliad* the thematic key to the *kléos áphthiton* of Achilles, while *Akhi-l(l)eús* is commensurately the key to the collective *ákhos* "grief" that the Achaeans have for Patroklos on the occasion of his funeral. Since this *ákhos* takes the social form of lamentations even within the epic of the *Iliad,* we can say that the theme we found in Pindar's *Isthmian* 8 is already active in the Homeric tradition; here too, lamentation extends into epic.

Up to now, I have been stressing the remoteness inherent in the concept of immortality after death, as we find it pictured in the formal discourse of the *thrênos* and then transposed into the narrative traditions of epic. In contrast to the remoteness of this immortality stands the stark immediacy of death, conveyed forcefully within the same medium of the *thrênos* and beyond. We are again reminded of the excerpt from the *thrênos* of Simonides, which says that even the *bíos* "lifespan" of the heroes themselves fails to be *áphthitos.* The latent vegetal imagery in this theme—that the life of man "wilts" like a plant—brings us now to yet another important contrast in the poetic representations of immortality and death. Traditional Hellenic poetry makes the opposition immortality/death not only remote/immediate but also artificial/natural. To put it another way: death and immortality are presented in terms of nature and culture respectively.

In *Iliad* book 6, Diomedes is about to attack Glaukos, but first he asks his opponent whether he is a god, not wishing at this time to fight an immortal (bk. 6, ll. 119–43; see the words for "mortal"/"immortal" at ll. 123, 142/128, 140, respectively). In response, Glaukos begins by saying:

> Son of Tydeus, you with the great *thūmós*! Why do you ask
> about my *geneē* [lineage, line of birth]?
> The *geneē* of men is like the *geneē* of leaves.
> Some leaves are shed on the earth by the wind,
> while others are grown by the greening forest—and the season
> of spring is at hand.
> So also the *geneē* of men: one grows, another wilts.
>
> (bk. 6, ll. 145–49)

Here the life and death of mortals are being overtly compared to a natural process, the growing and wilting of leaves on trees. In another such Homeric display of vegetal imagery, in this case spoken by the god Apollo himself as he talks about the human condition, this *natural* aspect of death is expressed specifically with the root *phthi-*:

> if I should fight you on account of mortals,
> the wretches, who are like leaves. At given times,
> they come to their fullness, bursting forth in radiance,
> eating the crops of the Earth,
> while at other times they wilt [*phthi-núthousin*], victims of fate.
>
> (bk. 21, ll. 463–66)

Let us straightway contrast the immortalized heroes on the Isles of the Blessed, whose abode flourishes with *golden* plant life. Also, let us contrast the First Generation of Mankind, whose very essence is gold. The immortality of the Golden Age is specifically correlated with the *suspension of a vegetal cycle*: in the Golden Age as on the Isles of the Blessed, the earth bears crops *without interruption*. The description of Elysium supplements this picture: in the state of immortality, there is simply *no winter,* nor any bad weather at all (*Odyssey,* bk. 4, ll. 566–68).

In these images, we see gold as a general symbol for the artificial continuum of immortality, in opposition to the natural cycle of life and death as symbolized by the flourishing and wilting of leaves on trees, where the theme of wilting is conventionally denoted with derivatives of the root *phthi-*. As we now set about to look for specific words that express this cultural negation of the vegetal cycle, we come back again to the negative epithet *áphthito-*. Let us begin with the *skêptron* "scepter" of Agamemnon (bk. 1, ll. 245–46), by which Achilles takes his mighty oath (bk. 1, ll. 234–44), and which is specifically described as "gold-studded" (χρυσείοις ἥλοισι πεπαρμένον: bk. 1, l. 246) and "golden" (χρυσέον: bk. 2, l. 268). This *skêptron,* by which Agamemnon holds sway in Argos (bk. 2, l. 108) and which an Achaean chieftain is bound by custom to hold in moments of solemn interchange (bk. 1, ll. 237–39; bk. 2, ll. 185–87), also qualifies specifically as *áphthiton aieí* "imperishable forever" (bk. 2, ll. 46 and 186). It was made by the ultimate craftsman, Hephaistos (bk. 2, l. 101), whose divine handicraft may be conventionally designated as both golden and *áphthito-* (e.g., bk. 14, ll. 238–39). Significantly, this everlasting artifact of a *skêptron* provides the basis for the Oath of Achilles in form as well as in function:

> But I will say to you and swear a great oath:
> I swear by this *skêptron,* which will no longer ever grow
>   leaves and shoots,
> ever since it has left its place where it was cut down
>   on the mountaintops—
> and it will never bloom again, for Bronze has trimmed
>   its leaves and bark.
> But now the sons of the Achaeans hold it in their hands
>   as they carry out *díkai.*
>
> (bk. 1, ll. 233–37)

Achilles is here swearing not only by the *skêptron* but also in terms of what the *skêptron* is—a thing of nature that has been transformed into a thing of culture. The Oath of Achilles is meant to be just as permanent and irreversible as the process of turning a shaft of living wood into a social artifact. And just as the *skêptron* is imperishable "*áphthiton,*" so also the Oath of Achilles is eternally valid, in that Agamemnon and the Achaeans will permanently regret not having given the hero of the *Iliad* his due *tīmḗ* (bk. 1, ll. 240–44).

For another Homeric instance featuring *áphthito-* as an epithet suitable for situations where the natural cycle of flourishing and wilting is negated, let us consider the Island of the Cyclopes. In *Odyssey* book 9, lines 116–41, this island and the mainland facing it are described in a manner that would suit the ideal Hellenic colony and its ideal *peraíā* respectively, if it were not for two special circumstances: the mainland is inhabited by Cyclopes, who are devoid of civilization (bk. 9, ll. 106–15), while the island itself is populated by no one at all—neither by humans nor even by Cyclopes, since they cannot navigate (ll. 123–25). At the very mention of navigation, there now follows a "what-if" narrative about the idealized place that the Island would become *if it were colonized* (ll. 126–29). If only there were ships (ll. 126–27), and these ships reached the Island, there would be commerce (ll. 127–29), and then there would also be agriculture, yielding limitless crops (ll. 130–35). What is more, the grapevines produced by this ideal never-never land would be *áphthitoi* "unfailing" (l. 133). Thus if culture rather than nature prevailed on the Island of the Cyclopes, then its local wine would bear the mark of immortality. Again we see the epithet *áphthito-* denoting permanence in terms of *culture* imposed on *nature*.

In fact, the epithet *áphthito-* functions as a mark of not only culture but even cult itself. In the Homeric *Hymn to Demeter* the infant Demophon is destined by the goddess to have a *tīmē* "cult" that is *áphthitos,* and this boon is contrasted directly with the certainty that he is *not* to avoid death. As Demophon's substitute mother, Demeter had actually been preparing him for a life that is never to be interrupted by death, but the inadvertence of the infant's real mother had brought that plan to naught. Still, Demophon is destined by the goddess to achieve immortality on the level of cult, so that her preparation of the infant was not in vain. We in fact catch a glimpse of the child's destiny as a hero of cult in the following description of how the goddess had been preparing him to be immortal:

> She nurtured him in the palace, and he grew up like a *daímōn*,
> not eating food, not sucking from the breast
>
> . . . .
>
> She used to anoint him with ambrosia, as if he had been born
> of the goddess,
> and she would breathe down her sweet breath on him
> as she held him at her bosom.
> At nights she would conceal him within the *ménos* of fire,
> as if he were a smoldering log,
> and his parents were kept unaware. But they marveled
> at how full in bloom he came to be, and to look at him
> was like looking at the gods.
> (*Hymn to Demeter,* ll. 235–36, 237–41)

The underscored phrase at verse 235, meaning "and he grew up like a *daímōn*," contains a word that we have in fact already seen in the specific function of designating heroes on the level of cult.

This same underscored phrase, as Sinos points out, has an important formal parallel in the *Iliad*.

> Ah me, the wretch! Ah me, the mother—so sad it is—
> of the very best.

I gave birth to a faultless and strong son,
the very best of heroes. <u>And he shot up like a seedling</u>.
I nurtured him like a shoot in the choicest spot
    of the orchard,
only to send him off on curved ships to fight at Troy. And
    I will never be welcoming him back home as
    returning warrior, back to the House of Peleus.
                                (bk. 18, ll. 54–60)

The context of these words is an actual lamentation (*góos*: bk. 18, l. 51),
sung by the mother of Achilles himself over the death of her son—a death
that is presupposed by the narrative from the very moment that the death of
the hero's surrogate Patroklos is announced to him.

It appears, then, that the mortality of a cult figure like Demophon is a
theme that calls for the same sort of vegetal imagery as is appropriate to the
mortality of Achilles. The examples can be multiplied: like the hero of the
Iliad, who is likened to a young shoot with words like *phutón* (bk. 18, ll. 57
and 438) and *ernos* (bk. 18, ll. 56 and 437), the hero of the *Hymn to Demeter* is
directly called a *néon thálos* "young sprout." Moreover, we have seen that
this theme of mortality common to Demophon and Achilles is replete with
the same sort of imagery that we find specifically in the genre of lamentation (consider again the *góos* of Thetis, bk. 18, ll. 54–60).

In this light, let us reconsider the epithet *áphthito-*. We have already seen
that it conveys the *cultural* negation of a *natural* process, the growing and the
wilting of plants, and also, by extension, the life and the death of mortals.
Now we must examine how this epithet conveys the theme of immortality in
its application to Demophon and Achilles as heroes of cult and epic respectively. As compensation for the death that he cannot escape, Demophon gets
a *tīmḗ* that is *áphthitos*; likewise, Achilles gets a *kléos* that is *áphthiton*. Thus
both heroes are destined for immortality in the form of a *cultural* institution
that is predicated on the *natural* process of death. For Demophon, this
predication is direct but implicit: by getting *tīmḗ* he is incorporated into hero
cult, a general institution that is implicitly built around the basic principle that
the hero must die. For the Achilles of our *Iliad,* this same predication is
explicit but indirect: by getting *kléos* he is incorporated into epic, which is
presented *by epic itself* as an eternal extension of the lamentation sung by the
Muses over the hero's death (*Odyssey,* bk. 24, ll. 60–61, 93–94). Thus the
specific institution of lamentation, which is an aspect of hero-cult and which
is implicit in the very name of Achilles, leads to the *kléos* of epic. For both
heroes, the key to immortality is the permanence of the cultural institutions

into which they are incorporated—cult for Demophon, epic for the Achilles of our *Iliad*. Both manifestations of both institutions qualify as *áphthito-*.

For the Achilles of our *Iliad*, the *kléos áphthiton* of epic (bk. 9, l. 413) offers not only an apparatus of heroic immortality but also a paradox about the human condition of the hero. Achilles himself says that the way for him to achieve this *kléos áphthiton* is to die at Troy (bk. 9, ll. 412–13), and that the way to lose *kléos* is to live life as a mortal, at home in *Phthíē* (bk. 9, ll. 413–16). The overt Iliadic contrast of *kléos áphthiton* with the negation of *kléos* in the context of *Phthíē* is remarkable in view of the element *phthi-* contained by the place name. From the wording of *Iliad* book 9, lines 412–16, we are led to suspect that this element *phthi-* is either a genuine formant of *Phthíē* or is at least perceived as such in the process of Homeric composition. We see the actual correlation of the intransitive verb *phthi-* (middle endings) "perish" with *Phthíē* at book 19, lines 328–30, where Achilles is wishing that he alone had died at Troy and that his surrogate Patroklos had lived to come home. Again, coming home to *Phthíē* (bk. 19, l. 330) is overtly contrasted with dying "*phthísesthai*" at Troy (bk. 19, l. 329). If indeed the name for the homeland of Achilles is motivated by the theme of vegetal death as conveyed by the root *phthi-*, then the traditional epithet reserved for the place is all the more remarkable: *Phthíē* is *bōtiáneira* "nourisher of men" (bk. 1, l. 155). The combination seems to produce a *coincidentia oppositorum*, in that the place name conveys the death of plants while its epithet conveys the life of plants— as it sustains the life of mortals. The element *bōti-* in this compound *bōti-áneira* stems from the verb system of *bóskō* "nourish," a word that specifically denotes the sustenance, *by vegetation*, of grazing animals, as at *Odyssey*, book 14, line 102, and of men, as at *Odyssey*, book 11, line 365. In the latter instance, the object of the verb *bóskei* "nourishes" is *anthrópous* "men," and the subject is actually *gaîa* "Earth." Thus the life and death of mortal men is based on the life and death of the plants that are grown for their nourishment: this is the message of the epithet *bōtiáneira* in its application to the homeland of Achilles. *Phthíē* is the hero's local Earth, offering him the natural cycle of life and death as an alternative to his permanent existence within the cultural medium of epic.

In the Homeric *Hymn to Demeter*, the foil for the permanence of cult as a cultural institution is also expressed by way of vegetal imagery: this time the image that we are considering is not the prolonged life but the prolonged death of plants, as denoted by the root *phthi-*. In contrast with the application of *áphthito-* to the *tīmḗ* of Demophon, let us consider the wording of the myth that tells how the permanence of all cult was endangered when the goddess Demeter prolonged indefinitely the failure of plant life:

> For she [Demeter] is performing a mighty deed,
> to destroy [*phthî-sai*] the tribes of earth-born men, causing them
>   to be without *ménos,*
> by hiding the Seed underground—and she is destroying [*kata-*
>   *phthinúthousa*] the *tīmaí* of the immortal gods.
>
> (*Hymn to Demeter,* ll. 351–54)

First, we are shown what the prolonged death of vegetation does to mortals, and we start with the adjective *amenēná* "without *ménos*" at line 352, derived from the noun *ménos* "power." This epithet is proleptic, in that it anticipates what Demeter does to mortals by virtue of taking away the sustenance of vegetation: she thereby takes away their *ménos,* and this action is here equated with the action of *phthîsai* at line 352, meaning "destroy" or, from the metaphorical standpoint of human life as plant life, "cause [plants] to fail." In Homeric diction, the intransitive uses of the same verb *phthi-* can designate the failing of wine supplies (*Odyssey,* bk. 9, l. 163) and of food supplies (*Odyssey,* bk. 12, l. 329); when the food supplies fail, *katéphthito,* the *ménea* of men who eat them fail also (*Odyssey,* bk. 4, l. 363). Second, we are shown what the prolonged death of vegetation does to the immortal gods: again, the action of Demeter is designated with the verb *phthi-* (*ka-taphthinúthousa,* line 353), but here the image of plant failure applies not to the gods directly but to their *tīmaí* "cults" instead. The impact of prolonged plant failure on cult is explicit:

> She [Demeter] would have completely destroyed the *génos*
>   of *méropes* men
> with the painful famine, and she would have taken away
>   from the gods who live in their Olympian abode
> the *tīmē* of honorific portions and sacrifices.
>
> (*Hymn to Demeter,* ll. 310–12)

We see, then, that the indefinite perpetuation of vegetal death as expressed by *phthi-* is a natural image of cosmic disorder; it functions as a foil for the cultural image of cosmic order, as represented by the indefinite perpetuation of vegetal life and as expressed by *áphthito-*. We also see now more clearly the suitability of this epithet *áphthito-* for the function of defining not only cult in particular but also the eternal cosmic apparatus of the immortal gods in general.

The cosmic order of the Olympians is of course not only *permanent* but also *sacred,* and in fact both these qualities are conveyed by the same epithet *áphthito-*. As we see from the Hesiodic tradition, nothing is more sacred or binding for the Olympians than taking an oath in the name of the Styx, and the river's waters in this particular context are specifically called *áphthito-*. If a god breaks such an oath, he has to endure the worst of punishments, which include the temporary withdrawal of divine sustenance, nectar and ambrosia. The children of the Styx, *Krátos* and *Bíē,* uphold the cosmic régime of Zeus, and in this context the river herself is called *áphthito-*. In the Homeric tradition as well (the *Hymns* included), to swear by the Styx is for any god the most sacrosanct of actions (bk. 15, ll. 37–39; *Odyssey,* bk. 5, ll. 185–86). When the goddess Demeter thus takes her oath in the name of the Styx, what she swears is that the infant Demophon would have had a life uninterrupted by death and a *tīmḗ* that is *áphthitos*. Demeter then says that the inadvertence of the infant's real mother has negated the first part of the Oath, but the second part remains valid: Demophon will still have a *tīmḗ* that is *áphthitos*. We now see that the epithet *áphthito-* in this context conveys not only the permanence of Demophon's cult, but also its intrinsic sacredness, as conferred by the essence of Demeter's Oath.

So also Achilles swears by the *skêptron* of King Agamemnon (bk. 1, ll. 234–39), affirming both that the Achaeans will one day yearn for him and that Agamemnon will then regret not having given "the best of the Achaeans" his due *tīmḗ* (bk. 1, ll. 240–44). Here we must keep in mind that the *skêptron* itself is *áphthiton* (bk. 2, ll. 46 and 186). Accordingly, the Oath of Achilles is not only permanent in its validity but also sacred. Moreover, the wish that the mother of Achilles conveys from the hero to Zeus is phrased from the standpoint of the Oath: let the Achaeans be hard pressed without the might of Achilles, and let their king regret not having given the hero his due *tīmḗ* (bk. 1, ll. 409–12). It is this wish that Thetis presents to Zeus (bk. 1, ll. 503–10), with special emphasis on the *tīmḗ* of Achilles (ll. 505, 507, 508, 510*bis*), and it is this wish that Zeus ratifies irrevocably (ll. 524–30). In this way, the Oath of Achilles is translated into the Will of Zeus, which, as we have seen, is the self-proclaimed plot of our *Iliad*. The oath is sacred because it is founded on the *skêptron,* which is *áphthiton*; now we see that the epic validating the *tīmḗ* of Achilles is also sacred, for the very reason that it is founded on this Oath. Accordingly, the epithet *áphthito-* as it applies to the *kléos* of Achilles (bk. 9, l. 413) conveys not only the permanence of the hero's epic but also its intrinsic sacredness as conferred by the essence of the hero's Oath.

The traditional application of *áphthito-* to both the cult of Demophon and the epic of Achilles serves as a key to what is for us a missing theme in the archaic story of Achilles. In the case of Demophon, we have seen how the hero gets a *tīmḗ* that is *áphthitos* because the goddess swears by the Styx, which is itself *áphthitos*. We have yet to follow through, however, on what such a combination of *Stúx* and *áphthitos* implies: *that the waters of the Styx are an elixir of life*. The lore about the cosmic stream Styx applies commensurately to the actual stream Styx in Arcadia, and in fact the belief prevails to this day that whoever drinks of that stream's waters *under the right conditions* may gain immortality. The point is that there survives for us a story telling how Thetis had immersed the infant Achilles into the waters of the Styx, in an unsuccessful attempt to exempt him from death. This failure of Thetis must be compared with the failure of Demeter in her attempt to make Demophon immortal. It would indeed by conventional for scholars to consider the story of Achilles in the Styx as a parallel to that of Demophon in the fire, if it were not for the fact that there is no attestation of such an Achilles story in archaic poetry. This obstacle may not perhaps be overcome with the indirect testimony of the epithet *áphthito-*: for both Demophon and Achilles, this word marks a compensatory form of immortality, and the Stygian authority of this deathlessness is overt in the case of Demophon. In the case of Achilles, we may say that the authority of the *skêptron* is a worthy variation on the authority of the *Stúx,* in that both *skêptron* and *Stúx* are intrinsically *áphthito-*. From the standpoint of diction, either could ratify the *kléos* of Achilles as *áphthiton*.

As our lengthy survey of the word *áphthito-* in Homeric and Hesiodic diction comes to an end, we conclude that this epithet can denote the permanent and sacred order of the Olympians, into which the hero is incorporated after death through such cultural media as epic in particular and cult in general.

It remains to ask a more important question: whether the theme of the hero immortalized in cult is compatible with the poetic visions of the hero immortalized by being transported to Elysium, to the Isles of the Blessed, or even to Olympus itself. Rohde, for one, thought that the concept of heroes being transported into a remote state of immortality is purely poetic and thus alien to the religious concept of heroes being venerated in cult. From the actual evidence of cult, however, we see that the two concepts are not at all treated as if they were at odds with each other. In fact, the forms *Elusion* "Elysium" and *Makárōn nêsoi* "Isles of the Blessed" are appropriate as names for actual cult sites. The proper noun *Ēlúsion* coincides with the common noun *en-ēlúsion*, meaning "place made sacred by virtue of being struck by the thunderbolt"; correspondingly, the adjective *en-ēlúsios* means "made sacred by virtue of being struck by the thunderbolt." The form *Ēlúsion* itself is glossed in the Alexandrian lexicographical tradition (Hesychius) as κεκεραυνωμένον χωρίον ἢ πεδίον "a place or field that has been struck by the thunderbolt," with this added remark: καλεῖται δὲ καὶ ἐνη-λύσια "and it is also called *enēlúsia*." As for *Makárōn nêsos,* there is a tradition that the name was actually applied to the old acropolis of Thebes, the Kadmeion; specifically, the name designated the sacred precinct where Semele, the mother of Dionysos, had been struck dead by the thunderbolt of Zeus. We are immediately reminded of the poetic tradition that tells how Semele became immortalized as a direct result of dying from the thunderbolt of Zeus.

We are in fact now ready to examine the general evidence of poetic traditions, in order to test whether the medium of poetry distinguishes this concept of heroes (or heroines) being transported into a state of immortality from the concept of their being venerated in cult. As with the evidence of cult itself, we will find that poetic diction reveals no contradiction between these two concepts.

Actually, there are poetic themes that tell of a hero's actual veneration in cult, and these themes are even combined with those that tell of his translation into immortality. Such combinations in fact form an integral picture of the heroic afterlife, as in the Hesiodic version of the Phaethon myth:

> And she [Eos] sprouted for Kephalos an illustrious son,
> sturdy Phaethon, a man who looked like the gods.
> When he was young and still had the tender bloom
>   of glorious adolescence,
> Aphrodite *philommeidḗs* rushed up and snatched him away
>   as he was thinking playful thoughts.
> And she made him an underground temple attendant, a *dîos*
>   *daímōn,* in her holy temple.
>
> (*Theogony,* ll. 986–91)

Phaethon in the afterlife is overtly presented as a *daímōn* of cult (l. 991) who functions within an undisturbed corner plot, *mukhós,* of Aphrodite's precinct (hence *múkhios* at l. 991) as the goddess's *nēopólos* "temple attendant" (again l. 991). The designation of Phaethon as *daímōn* also conveys the immortal aspect of the hero in his afterlife, since it puts him in the same category as the Golden Generation, who are themselves explicitly *daímones.* As for the mortal aspect of Phaethon, we may observe the vegetal imagery surrounding his birth and adolescence. When he is about to be snatched away forever, he bears the *ánthos* "bloom" of adolescence. Earlier, the verb that denotes his very birth from Eos is *phītū́sato:* the Dawn Goddess "sprouted" him as if he were some plant. We see here in the *Theogony* the only application of *phītúein* "sprout" to the act of reproduction, which is elsewhere conventionally denoted by *tíktein* and *geínasthai*. The most immediate parallel is the birth of the Athenian hero Erekhtheus, who was directly sprouted by Earth herself:

> Athena the daughter of Zeus once upon a time
> nurtured him, but grain-giving earth gave him birth,
> and she [Athena] established him in Athens,
>> in her own rich temple,
> and there it is that the *koûroi* of the Athenians supplicate him,
> every year when the time comes, with bulls and lambs.
>> (bk. 2, ll. 547–51)

As with Phaethon, the immortal aspect of the hero Erekhtheus is conveyed by his permanent installation within the sacred precinct of a goddess.

We have yet to examine the actual process of Phaethon's translation into heroic immortality. The key word is the participle *anereipsaménē*, describing Aphrodite at the moment that she snatches Phaethon away to be with her forever. The word recurs in the finite form *anēreípsanto* (bk. 20, l. 234), describing the gods as they abduct Ganymedes to be the cup bearer of Zeus for all time to come. In the next verse, we hear the motive for the divine action:

> on account of his beauty, so that he might be
>> among the Immortals.
>> (bk. 20, l. 235)

The Homeric *Hymn to Aphrodite* elaborates on the same myth: it was Zeus himself who abducted Ganymedes. Here too, the motive is presented as the same:

> on account of his beauty, so that he might be
>> among the Immortals.
>> (*Hymn to Aphrodite*, l. 203)

In this retelling as well as in all the others, Ganymedes becomes the cup bearer of Zeus; *and as such he abides in the gods' royal palace at Olympus*. By virtue of gaining Olympian status, he is in fact described as an Immortal himself:

> immortal and unaging, just as the gods are.
>> (*Hymn to Aphrodite*, l. 214)

As cup bearer and boy-love of Zeus, Ganymedes also qualifies as a *daímōn*:

> Loving a boy is a pleasant thing. For even the Son of Kronos,
> king of the Immortals, loved Ganymedes.
> He abducted him, took him up to Olympus, and made him
> a *daímōn*, having the lovely bloom of boyhood.

The parallelisms between this Theognidean passage about Ganymedes and the Hesiodic passage about Phaethon are remarkable not just because of the convergences in detail (both heroes are described as *daímōn*, both have the *ánthos* "bloom" of youth, etc.). An even more remarkable fact about these parallelisms is that the processes of *preservation on Olympus* and *preservation in cult* function as equivalent poetic themes.

The parallelisms between the myth of Ganymedes and that of Phaethon lead to our discovery of further details about the process of heroic preservation. When the gods abducted *"anēreípsanto"* the young Ganymedes (bk. 20, l. 234), the specific instrument of the divine action was a gust of wind, an *áella*:

> to whatever place the wondrous *áella* abducted him.
> (*Hymn to Aphrodite*, l. 208)

Actually, in every other Homeric attestation of *anēreípsanto* besides book 20, line 234, the notion "gusts of wind" serves as subject of the verb. When Penelope mourns the unknown fate of her absent son Telemachus, she says:

> But now the *thúellai* have abducted my beloved son.
> (*Odyssey*, bk. 4, l. 727)

When Telemachus mourns the unknown fate of his absent father Odysseus, he says:

> But now the *hárpuiai* have abducted him, without *kléos*.
> (*Odyssey*, bk. 1, l. 241)

The meaning of *thúella* "gust of wind" is certain (see the collocation of *thúella* with *anémoio* "of wind" at bk. 6, l. 346, etc.). As for *hárpuia*, a word that is also personified as "Harpy," the same meaning "gust of wind" is apparent from the only remaining Homeric attestation of the verb *anēreípsanto* "abducted." After Penelope wishes that Artemis smite her dead and take her *thūmós* immediately, we hear her make an alternative wish:

> or later, may a *thúella* abduct me;
> may it go off and take me away along misty ways,
> and plunge me into the streams of Okeanos, which flows
>   in a circle.
> (*Odyssey*, bk. 20, ll. 63–65)

As precedent for being abducted by a gust of wind and cast down into the Okeanos, her words evoke the story about the daughters of Pandareos:

> as when the *thúellai* took away the daughters of Pandareos.
> (*Odyssey*, bk. 20, l. 66)

This mention of abduction is followed by a description of how the Pandareids were preserved by the Olympian goddesses (ll. 67–72). The preservation of the girls is then interrupted by death, at the very moment that Aphrodite is arranging for them to be married (ll. 73–74). Death comes in the form of abduction:

> then the *hárpuiai* abducted the girls.
> (*Odyssey*, bk. 20, l. 77)

Our survey has by now covered all the Homeric/Hesiodic attestations of *anēreípsanto/anereipsaménē*, and we can reach several conclusions. Most important of all, we see that the divine abduction of mortals by gusts of wind (*thúellai* or *hárpuiai*) entails not only preservation but also sex and death. Of these last two experiences, we will leave the first in abeyance until we confront the second.

In the imagery of passages featuring the forms *anēreípsanto/anereipsaménē*, you experience death when the abducting winds plunge you into the earth-encircling river Okeanos. So we have seen from Penelope's death wish (*Odyssey*, bk. 20, ll. 63–65). As we see further from Homeric diction, especially at *Odyssey*, book 24, lines 1–14, the Okeanos is one of the prime mythical boundaries that serve to delimit light from darkness, life from death, wakefulness from sleep, consciousness from unconsciousness. The River Okeanos marks the cosmic extremities beyond Earth and Seas (cf. bk. 14, ll. 301–2). The Sun himself, Helios, plunges into it every sunset (bk. 8, l. 485) and emerges from it every sunrise (bk. 7, ll. 421–23; *Odyssey*, bk. 19, ll. 433–34). As the Sun thus rises at Dawn from the Okeanos, he stirs the *árourai* "fertile lands" (bk. 7, l. 421; *Odyssey*, bk. 19, l. 433), and we are reminded by this action that the noun *ároura* itself traditionally attracts such epithets of fertility as *zeídōros* "grain-giving" (bk. 2, l. 548; bk. 8, l. 486, etc.). Since plunging into the Okeanos overtly conveys death (*Odyssey*, bk. 20, ll. 63–65), it follows that the notion of emerging from it conveys regeneration. For the Sun, we infer that regeneration through Okeanos is cosmic, bringing with it the fertility of Earth itself; in fact, Okeanos qualifies not only as *theôn génesin* "genesis of gods" (bk. 14, ll. 201 and 302) but even as *génesis pántessi* "genesis for all things" (bk. 14, l. 246).

In this light, it becomes significant that the Okeanos is also a traditional landmark both for the Isles of the Blessed and for Elysium itself (*Odyssey*, bk. 4, ll. 567–68). What is more, the Okeanos in the context of Elysium has the specific function of reanimating mortals:

> but the Okeanos sends up gusts of shrill-blowing Zephyros
> at all times, so as to reanimate men.
>
> (*Odyssey,* bk. 4, ll. 567–68)

On the basis, then, of incidental references to the Sun and its movements in epic diction, we can detect a solar model of death and regeneration—both through the Okeanos. Moreover, we see that this solar model applies to the general theme of the hero's return from death. As we now look for specific instances of this theme, we turn to the myths about the personification of sunrise, Eos. In doing so we also confront a third theme in the myths of abduction: having already noted death and preservation, we are ready to reckon with a theme of sex.

There is an archaic tradition that features the Dawn Goddess Eos herself abducting young male mortals, and her motive is in part sexual. In the *Odyssey,* the immortal nymph Kalypso cites the abduction of Orion by Eos as a precedent for her mating with Odysseus (bk. 5, ll. 121–24). Similarly, Aphrodite herself cites both the abduction of Ganymedes by Zeus *and the abduction of Tithonos by Eos* as precedents for her mating with Anchises. As for the abduction of Phaethon, again by Aphrodite, the precedent is built into the young hero's genealogy: his father Kephalos had been abducted by his mother Eos.

As with the myth of Aphrodite and Phaethon, the myths of Eos too are marked by the design of making the hero immortal. Thus when Eos abducts Kleitos, her motive is described in these words:

> on account of his beauty, so that he might be
> among the Immortals.
>
> (*Odyssey,* bk. 15, l. 251)

The very same words, as we have seen, mark the immortalization of Ganymedes after his abduction by Zeus. The divine motive for abduction by Eos is thus both preservative and sexual.

In order to see at a closer range the operation of a solar model in the myths of divine abduction, let us return to the Hesiodic myth of Phaethon. The form of his name in Homeric diction serves as an actual epithet of *Hḗlios* the Sun (as at bk. 11, l. 735). What is more, his mother is *Eṓs* the Dawn, while the goddess who abducted him embodies regeneration itself, Aphrodite.

On the level of celestial dynamics, these associations imply the theme of a setting sun mating with the goddess of regeneration so that the rising sun may be reborn. Let us pursue this scheme—so far hypothetical only—one step further: if the setting sun is the same as the rising sun, then the goddess of regeneration may be viewed as both mate and mother. Such an ambivalent relationship actually survives in the hymns of the *Rig-Veda,* where the goddess of solar regeneration, Uṣas- "Dawn," is the wife or bride of the sun god Sūrya- as well as his mother (*RV* 7.63.3, 7.78.3). In the latter instance, the incestuous implications are attenuated by putting Uṣas- into the plural, representing a succession of dawns. Similarly, Uṣas- in the plural can designate the wives of Sūrya-. Yet even if each succeeding dawn is wife of the preceding dawn's son, the husband and son are always one and the same Sūrya-, and the basic theme of incest remains.

There is more than one reason for comparing these Indic traditions about Sūrya- "Sun" and Uṣas- "Dawn" to such Greek traditions as we see in the myth of Phaethon. First and most obvious, the actual forms Sūrya- and Uṣas- are cognate with *Hélios* "Sun" and *Ēós* "Dawn." Second, there are instances in Homeric diction where the relationship of the forms *Ēós* and *Phaéthōn* is directly parallel to the relationship of Rig-Vedic Uṣas- and Sūrya-. Besides being an epithet of *Hélios* (bk. 11, l. 735, etc.), the form *Phaéthōn* also functions as a name for one of the two horses of *Ēós*:

> *Lámpos* and *Phaéthōn,* who are the horses that pull *Ēós.*
> (*Odyssey,* bk. 23, l. 246)

We may note that *Lámpos,* the name of her other horse, is also associated with the notion of brightness. The Rig-Vedic parallel here is that Sūrya- the sun god is called the "bright horse," *śvetám . . . áśvam,* of the Dawn Goddess Uṣas-. There is also, within Homeric diction itself, an internal analogue to the combination of *Phaéthōn* and *Lámpos* at *Odyssey,* book 23, line 246. The names for the daughters of *Hélios* the sun god are *Phaéthousa* and *Lampetíē* (*Odyssey,* bk. 12, l. 132), which are feminine equivalents of *Phaéthōn* and *Lámpos.* The Rig-Vedic parallel here is that the name for the daughter of Sūrya- the sun god is Sūryā, a feminine equivalent of the masculine name. The comparative evidence of this contextual nexus suggests that the Horses of the Dawn at *Odyssey,* book 23, line 246 had once been metaphorical aspects of the Sun. As in the *Rig-Veda,* the Sun could have been called the bright horse of the Dawn—by such names as *Phaéthōn* or *Lámpos.* Once the metaphor is suspended, then the notion "Horse of the Dawn" becomes reorganized: if the Dawn has a horse, she will actually have not one but two for a chariot team, and the two kindred solar aspects *Phaéthōn* "bright" and *Lámpos* "bright" will do nicely as names for two distinct horses. Yet the surviving function of *Phaéthousa* and *Lampetíē* as daughters of Helios serves as testimony for the eroded personal connotations of the names *Phaéthōn* and *Lámpos*. By contrast, the metaphor is maintained in the *Rig-Veda*, where Sūrya- the sun god is both bridegroom and horse of the dawn goddess Uṣas-. There is even a special word that conveys both functions of Sūrya-, namely *márya-*. In fact, the metaphorical equation of horse and bridegroom is built into various rituals of Indic society, such as that of initiation, and a key to this equation is the same word *márya-* and its Iranian cognate.

Significantly, there is a corresponding Greek attestation of such a metaphorical equation, in the context of a wedding song:

> Hymen, Hymen!
> We sing the celestial daughter of Zeus,
> the Mistress of Love, the one who gets maidens united
>   in matrimony, Aphrodite.
> My Lady, I sing this wedding song to you,
> O Kypris, most beautiful of gods!
> —and also to your newly yoked
> *pôlos* [horse], the one you hide in the aether,
> the offspring of your wedding.
>   (Euripides, *Phaethon*, ll. 227–35D)

The *pôlos* "horse" of Aphrodite is Hymen himself, and we note that the same word at *Odyssey*, book 23, line 246 designates the horses of Eos, Phaethon and Lampos. We also note that Hymen's epithet νεόζυγι "newly yoked" (l. 233) marks him as Aphrodite's bridegroom. As for the appositive σῶν γάμων γένναν "offspring of your wedding" (l. 235), it conveys that Hymen is also Aphrodite's son. We must at the same time appreciate that this entire wedding song to Aphrodite and Hymen is being sung in honor of *Phaéthōn*, and that his bride-to-be is in all probability a daughter of the Sun. Finally, we note that Aphrodite here functions as τὰν Διὸς οὐρα-νίαν "the celestial daughter of Zeus" (l. 228). This characterization now brings us to a third important reason for comparing the Indic traditions about Sūrya- "Sun" and Uṣas- "Dawn" with the Greek traditions about *Phaéthōn* and *Ēôs*.

The epithets of Uṣas- "Dawn" in the *Rig-Veda* prominently include *divá(s) duhitár-* and *duhitár- divás* "Daughter of Sky"—exact formal cognates of the Homeric epithets *Diòs thugátēr* and *thugátēr Diós* "Daughter of Zeus." In the surviving traditions of Greek poetry, however, this epithet is assigned not to Eos herself but to Aphrodite and other goddesses. When these goddesses qualify as *Diòs thugátēr/thugátēr Diós,* they fulfill the inherited functions of Eos herself, and nowhere is this more apparent than in the story of Aphrodite and Anchises. We have already seen that when Aphrodite seduces the young hero, she herself cites the abduction of Tithonos by Eos as precedent. Now we may add that throughout the seduction episode, Aphrodite is actually called *Diòs thugátēr.*

The replacement of Eos as *Diòs thugátēr/thugátēr Diós* by Aphrodite and other goddesses leads to a fragmentation of her original functions. From the comparative evidence of the *Rig-Veda,* we might have expected Eos to be both the mother and the consort of a solar figure like Phaethon. Instead, the Hesiodic tradition assigns Aphrodite as consort of Phaethon, while Eos is only his mother. We may infer that the originally fused functions of mating with the consort and being reborn from the mother were split and divided between Aphrodite and Eos respectively. However, such a split leaves Phaethon as son of Eos simply by birth rather than by rebirth.

For another instance of fragmentation in the functions of Eos, let us consider what happens to the originally fused functions of abduction, death, and preservation in the myth of Orion at *Odyssey,* book 5, lines 121–24: here Eos abducts and preserves the young hero Orion, but then he is killed by Artemis. I infer that the function of causing the death of Orion had been reassigned from Eos to Artemis. In this same function of causing death, Artemis actually qualifies as *thúgater Diós* (vocative) in Penelope's death wish (*Odyssey,* bk. 20, 1. 61). Eos, on the other hand, retains the function of abducting and preserving Orion. Accordingly, the Orion myth is marked by the sequence *abduction/preservation followed by death*; this pattern is the inverse of *abduction/death followed by preservation*—the sequence that marks the myth of Phaethon.

In contrast to the solar myth of Phaethon, the inverse sequence that marks the myth of Orion results in a scheme that is astral. We may note that the figure of Orion is in fact already an astral image in Homeric diction (bk. 18, 1. 488; *Odyssey,* bk. 5, 1. 274), and that the relation of Orion's celestial movements to the Dawn is the inverse of the Sun's movements. Like the Sun, the constellation Orion rises from the Okeanos and sets in it (bk. 18, 1. 489; bk. 5, 1. 275). Unlike the Sun, it rises and sets at night, not in daytime. In the summer, at threshing time, Orion starts rising before Dawn. In the winter, at ploughing time, Orion starts setting before Dawn. In summer days, the light of Dawn catches up with the rising Orion, and he can be her consort in the daytime. In winter days, the light of Dawn arrives too late to keep Orion from setting into the Okeanos.

One related star which does not set, however, is the *Árktos* "Bear":

> She alone has no share in the baths of Okeanos.
> (bk. 18, l. 489 and *Odyssey*, bk. 5, l. 275)

Since the theme of plunging into the Okeanos conveys the process of death (see again bk. 20, ll. 63–65), it follows that the exemption of Arktos from ever having to set into the Okeanos conveys her immortality. The Arktos "stalks Orion," *Ōríōna dokeúei* (bk. 18, l. 488 and *Odyssey*, bk. 5, l. 274), and the verb *dokeúei* "stalks" implies doom. In Homeric diction, it applies when marksmen or beasts take aim at their victims (bk. 13, l. 545, bk. 16, l. 313, bk. 8, l. 340). In the lore reported by Pausanias, the name *Árktos* applies also to Kallisto as mother of Arkas and hence progenitrix of the Arkades "Arcadians"; she is represented as being turned into a bear and being killed by Artemis. The heroine *Kallistō* herself is the ritual antagonist of Artemis *Kallístē*, whose sanctuary is located on the "Mound of Kallisto." On the basis of such traditions, featuring an intimate nexus between Artemis and the concept of *Árktos*, we are encouraged to infer an actual identification in the astral scheme: an immortal Arktos stalks a mortal Orion at book 18, lines 487–89 and *Odyssey*, book 5, lines 273–75, and the image implicitly retells the myth of Artemis killing Orion, explicit at *Odyssey*, book 5, lines 121–24. As Odysseus is floating along on his nocturnal sea voyage, he contemplates this image of Arktos stalking Orion in the sky above (*Odyssey*, bk. 5, ll. 271–75), which Kalypso had marked out for him to fix the direction in which his raft is to sail (ll. 276–77). Since Kalypso herself had compared her seduction of Odysseus with the abduction of Orion by Eos (l. 121), the connected theme of Orion's death from the shafts of Artemis (ll. 122–24) makes the image of Arktos stalking Orion at lines 271–75 an ominous sign indeed for Odysseus. He is being guided away from the Island of Kalypso by a celestial sign that points to the fate awaiting him if he had stayed behind as bedmate of the immortal goddess.

Such is the power of a myth that results ultimately from the fragmentation of the functions once encompassed by one figure, the pre-Olympian goddess Eos. It is through this figure that we can better appreciate the traditional nature not only of myths concerned with the immortalization of the hero but also of sundry other myths concerned with how this process can go wrong.

Of course, it scarcely needs saying that we have so far managed to cover merely one type of myth concerning the immortalization of the hero. Besides this type, which centers on the theme of abduction by winds, there are doubtless other major types with other themes, other details. Here is my tentative list, surely incomplete, of alternative ways for the hero to achieve immortality:

- being struck by a thunderbolt of Zeus
- plunging from a white rock into the deep waters below
- being suddenly engulfed by the Earth.

Ideally, we could embark on a detailed survey of these additional types, but it will suffice for us now to draw inferences from the model featuring abduction by Eos or by the divine figures that replaced her functions. Even in the case of this model, however, I dare make no claim that we have seen the whole picture. Every additional attestation would serve to enhance and even alter our perception of Eos and how she confers immortality on the hero.

This much, in any case, can be said with some confidence: the functions of Eos that prevail in the Greek myths have been by and large restricted to beneficent ones, in that we find her consistently promoting the immortality of the hero. The functions associated with her inherited epithet, on the other hand, remain ambivalent. We have already noted that this epithet, *Diòs thugátēr/thugátēr Diós,* along with its thematic associations, has been reassigned to other goddesses, who are thereby endowed with maleficent as well as beneficent functions. The clearest example of the maleficent aspect in Homeric diction is the passage where Penelope prays to Artemis for death, invoking her in this context as *thúgater Diós* (*Odyssey,* bk. 20, l. 61). As for the beneficent aspect, there are many examples available, and most of them are suited—no surprise—to the particular requirements of epic narrative. For instance, Athena qualifies as *Diòs thugátēr* (bk. 4, l. 128) when she rescues Menelaos from certain death on the battlefield (bk. 4, ll. 127–30); in this context, she is specifically compared to a mother fostering her child (bk. 4, ll. 130–31). This function of the *Diòs thugátēr* as a motherly goddess who preserves the hero from mortal harm is typical on the level of epic narrative. On a more fundamental level, however, this function of *Diòs thugátēr* entails not only the temporary preservation of the hero in epic action but also his permanent preservatoin in the afterlife. There is actually an important attestation of this basic function in epic action. Even more important, the goddess in question is not some derivative *Diòs thugátēr* but Eos herself. The only surviving attestation of her taking a direct part in epic action is the *Aithiopis,* where she translates her dead son Memnon into a state of immortality.

The heroic figure Memnon, even within epic action, is ideally suited for this theme of immortalization, since tradition makes him not only son of Eos but also king of the Aithiopes. The kingdom of the Aithiopes is situated on the banks of the Okeanos, and the Olympian gods themselves habitually go all the way to the Okeanos in order to receive sacrifice from them (bk. 1, ll. 423–24; bk. 23, ll. 205–7; *Odyssey,* bk. 1, ll. 22–26). And just as the world-encircling Okeanos flows in the extreme East and the extreme West, so also the kingdom of the Aithiopes is situated in the two extremities:

> the Aithiopes, who are divided in two, the most remote of men:
> some where Hyperion [Helios] sets, others where he rises.
>
> (*Odyssey,* bk. 1, ll. 23–24)

This instance of *coincidential oppositorum,* where identity consists of two opposites, has an interesting parallel involving Okeanos and Eos directly. Again we are about to see how two opposite places can add up to the same place. To begin, from the overall plot of the *Odyssey,* we know that Odysseus is wandering in the realms of the extreme West when he comes upon the island of Aiaia (*Odyssey,* bk. 10, l. 135). It is from Aiaia, island of Circe, that Odysseus is sent on his way to the underworld by traveling beyond the sea until he and his men reach the cosmic river Okeanos (*Odyssey,* bk. 11, ll. 21–22). Later, on the way back from the underworld, the ship of Odysseus has to leave the Okeanos before returning to Aiaia, which is now described as situated not in the extreme West but in the extreme East. In fact, Aiaia now turns out to be the abode of Eos and sunrise:

> But when the ship left the stream of the river Okeanos,
> and reached the waves of the sea with its wide-flung paths,
> and then the Island Aiaia—and there are the abode
>   and the dancing places
> of early-born Eos, and the sunrises of Helios.
>
> (*Odyssey,* bk. 12, ll. 1–4)

In short, the Okeanos in the extreme East is a key to the emergence of Odysseus from his sojourn in the world of the dead—a sojourn that began when he reached the Okeanos in the extreme West.

By being king of the realms along the banks of the Okeanos in the extreme East and West, the figure of Memnon is implicitly associated with a whole set of themes that center on the immortalization of the hero. We are reminded that Elysium itself is situated on the banks of the Okeanos, from which the wind Zephyros blows to reanimate mortals (*Odyssey,* bk. 4, ll. 567–68). So too are the Isles of the Blessed, where heroes who fought and died in the Trojan War were translated through the ultimate agency of Zeus. We see the same agency at work in the *Aithiopis,* when Eos herself asks the permission of Zeus that she may give immortality to her fallen son Memnon. The *Aithiopis* also has an important parallel to the action of Eos: the immortal Thetis translates her own son Achilles from a state of death into a state of immortality on the Island of Leuke. To my mind, it is useless to argue, on the basis of such parallels, that the immortalization of Achilles was modeled on the immortalization of Memnon. All that matters is that both are traditional themes that fit the essence of the hero in cult, and that both also fit the general pattern of the afterlife in store for the Fourth Generation of Mankind.

Having returned to the Hesiodic Myth of the Five Generations of Mankind, we may conclude this chapter with the same theme that inaugurated [another] one. By now we see that the process of immortalization that comes after Generation IV is an essential link with the idyllic state of Generation I. Thus the picture of the hero in epic, as seen in Generations III/IV, can revert to the picture of the hero in cult, as seen in Generations I/II. Even the most stylized hero of epic may get his due in cult, and in that spirit I close with two examples.

For the first example, I choose a bit of lore from the Hellespont. As Pausanias surveys the paintings of Polygnotus in the Knidian Lesche at Delphi, his attention is suddenly riveted on a detail as he describes the picture of Memnon. On the hero's cloak are images of birds:

> And *Memnonídes* is the name of the birds. The people of the Hellespont say that every year on certain days these birds go to Memnon's grave, and where the grave is bare of trees or grass the birds sweep through it and sprinkle it with their wings, which are wet with the water of the Aisepos.

From this information, however fragmentary it may be, we discover that even a hero who has been translated into a remote state of immortality is traditionally eligible to have not only a cult but even a grave or funeral mound.

Of course, myths about the immortalization of a hero imply that his *body* has been regenerated, as we see from the application of the word *autós* "himself" to the immortalized Herakles who abides on Olympus (*Odyssey*, bk. 11, l. 602). In Homeric diction, *autós* designates the hero's *body* after death (as in bk. 1, l. 4), in comparison to his *psūkhḗ*, which travels to Hades (as in bk. 1, l. 3). Accordingly, the hero's remains cannot be pictured as being in his grave *once he is immortalized,* and there seems at first glance to be a conflict here with the requirements of cult, the original basis for which is the belief that the hero's bones are buried in his grave. Unlike others, however, I see no conflict *so long as the promise of immortalization aims not at the here-and-now but rather at a fulfillment in the hero's future.* If this condition holds, then the ultimate aspect of the afterlife, from the standpoint of both cult and myth, turns out to be not

Hades but rather Elysium, the Isles of the Blessed, and all the other variations on the theme of immortalization. Hades, on the other hand, would be the transitional aspect of the afterlife, when the *psūkhē* is separated from the body. Then, in a place like Elysium, body and *psūkhē* can be reintegrated when the Zephyros blows from the Okeanos to *reanimate* men—the word for which is *anapsūkhein* (*Odyssey*, bk. 4, l. 568).

In fact, the traditional emphasis on the hero's bones in cult represents a formal commitment to the promise of immortalization. The discipline of anthropology can help us here, with its vast reservoir of experience about parallel social institutions, taken from actual field work. On the basis of innumerable typological parallels as surveyed by Karl Meuli and his followers, we now know that the function of bones in Hellenic cult and myth is to symbolize the ultimate regeneration not only of sacrificial animals but also of mortal men themselves. One of the prime models for this process of regeneration by way of dismembered bones is the god Dionysos himself. It is beyond my scope to offer even the briefest survey here of the themes and the sources, but I must still mention an important application of the Dionysiac model to the immortalization of Achilles himself. This particular application can bring us to my second example showing how an immortalized hero, no matter how stylized he may have become in the medium of epic, may still be envisioned in a context that pertains to the medium of cult.

From Stesichorus, we know of a tradition that Dionysos had given a golden amphora, made by Hephaistos, to the goddess Thetis, in compensation for her having preserved him after he fled from Lykourgos by plunging into the sea (cf. bk. 6, ll. 130–40). It is into this same golden amphora that the bones of Achilles were placed, together with those of his surrogate Patroklos, on the occasion of his funeral (*Odyssey*, bk. 24, ll. 72–76; cf. bk. 23, ll. 91–92). From what we know about the symbolic function of bones in general and about regeneration in particular, we may see in this formal token the promise of an ultimate immortality in store for the hero of the *Iliad*.

Formula and Foreground:
Homer and the Dipylon Style

Jeffrey M. Hurwit

Just before the middle of the eighth century, one of Athens's leading families awarded an important commission to one of the city's handful of potter's workshops. A noblewoman (the family's matriarch?) had just died or was about to die, and a gigantic vase was required to stand over her grave in a cemetery not far from the later city gate known as the Dipylon (Double Door). The vase could receive libations poured by mourners, but its function was essentially commemorative: it was both the sign (*sēma*) of the noblewoman's tomb and her memorial (*mnēma*), a monument of remembrance.

Tradition determined the type of vase it was to be. In the preceding centuries, when Athenians generally cremated their dead, the ashes of women were buried in belly-handled amphorae. Now, when inhumation had become the preferred form of burial, the remains of women rested beneath such amphorae rather than in them. There is no way of knowing whether the aristocrat who arranged the funeral provided the potter with any other specifications concerning size or decoration; he would, perhaps, have been a rare patron if he did not. At all events, although large vases had marked graves before, no earlier Greek potter had ever undertaken a task so monumental as this. He began by throwing prepared clay on his wheel and directed the rising, spreading form as an apprentice spun the wheel by hand. The vase was actually too large to be thrown all at once, so the potter made it in sections. That task done, he literally built the vase, binding the parts together

From *The Art and Culture of Early Greece, 1100–480 B.C.* © 1985 by Cornell University. Cornell University Press, 1985.

with a clay slip, carefully smoothing the seams. He left undisguised the sharp angle where the swelling egg-shaped body meets the cylindrical, slightly flaring neck. The finished product stood just over five feet tall (1.55 m)—the scale of a human being—and it was constructed according to a precise proportional scheme: it is twice as tall as it is wide, the neck is half the height of the body. The master potter lastly added two double-looping handles and set the monument aside to dry and stiffen. Then he turned master draftsman and, with a fine solution of clay and water that would turn dark only after the vase was fired, began to paint.

A lot had happened in Attic vase painting since the Middle Geometric I mourner took her inconspicuous and independent place beyond the borders of a complex geometric world. That first Attic human figure precipitated a mighty confrontation between the pictorial and the abstract, and in the following decades the pictorial slowly gained strength. During the Middle Geometric II period (800–760) figures were not only painted on vases but also engraved on the flat catch plates of gold brooches (fibulae). Counting these engravings, the Attic repertoire of images expanded to include horses, birds, deer (standing or grazing), a family of pigs, a goat, a lion, and ships (the vehicle of much Athenian prosperity in those years). But the crucial development in Middle Geometric II picture making was the final acknowledgment of the inherent attractions of the human form.

Human beings no longer appear alone: they are grouped with other human beings and the relationships between them begin to be described. That is, while the Middle Geometric I mourner and the nearby horse are merely forlorn abbreviations of human activity (in that case, a funeral), Middle Geometric II artists represent true "scenes." Broad-shouldered men tame a horse with whip and reins. Rubbery-limbed warriors fight on land and sea, defending and attacking beached ships: some hurl spears, some crouch and take aim with bows, some duel with swords, some fall and die. Such scenes are often ambiguous in content and in the representation of space (some figures hover in midair), but they are surprisingly energetic and are thus early manifestations of the characteristically Attic impulse for dynamic narrative. They also record the kinds of action that undoubtedly won Athenian aristocrats considerable glory in the early eighth century and that made them more like the heroes epic poets were singing about. One battle completely girds the belly of a monumental krater in New York—the *mnēma* of a nobleman who died around 770—and it may stand for ("illustrate" would be the wrong word) a glorious episode in the life of the deceased or even the occasion of his death. On a decorative band above, in the middle of the handle zone, there is a badly damaged representation of a *prothesis* (the highly patterned ritual that included the lying in state of the corpse), the first of hundreds in Geometric art. A mourner kneels atop the funerary couch at the feet of the dead. Below the bier is a file of birds and lower still, in a separate register, are five mourners. There are more figures below the handles of the vase; this is the large, aggrieved company that the Middle Geometric I mourner had to suggest all by herself. In fact, these figures look like her direct descendants: their arms curl over their heads, their contours are fluid and fleshy. But unlike her, the Middle Geometric II figures have passed from the edge of the abstract labyrinth to its very center. They have acquired a frame, a secure place, and have been brought within the ordered Geometric world. With that move the Dark Age of Greek art came to an end. The human figure never gave up the center again.

And yet there was a problem. If the Attic vase painter had concluded that the future lay in pictures, he was not yet clear how (or whether) to integrate them with their abstract environment. The painter of the cup from Eleusis skirted the issue almost entirely: he surrounded his battles with solid black glaze, not geometric ornament. On the New York krater the issue is addressed but not completely resolved: the *prothesis* panel seems like a light hole rent in the abstract fabric, and the picture thus threatens the integrity of the surface. The vase painter had two choices now: either he could give the surface over to the pictorial once and for all and make mere borders of geometric designs or, more conservatively, he could minimize the inherent (and unfair) competition between the pictorial and the abstract by making the human figure into another geometric motif and transforming the representation into half-abstract pattern. Ultimately, Greek artists made the first choice. But the master potter and painter who received that special aristocratic commission around 760–50 made the second. With the great vase he constructed and decorated—Athens 804, as it is known—the Late Geometric style essentially began and Greek art acquired its first recognizable personality: the Dipylon Master.

Leaving representation aside for the moment, the history of Geometric vase painting had consisted of balancing rigid organization with the gradual expansion of decorative zones. Athens 804 is the monumental culmination of the process: it is covered with ornament from its top nearly to its (reconstructed) bottom. At first glance, the surface is a bewildering display of abstract motifs. In fact, the motifs are traditional and the surface is controlled by visual rhythms and formulae. The simplest formula is a band of three (sometimes two) thin horizontal lines: it is so common (on the front of the vase it appears nearly fifty times, if the vertical strips between the handles are counted) that it binds together the larger building blocks of the surface like geometric mortar (or, to mix metaphors, stitching). The triple-line band is combined with other patterns to form more complex formulae: the formula triple-line band/dotted lozenge frieze/triple-line band, for instance, occurs eleven times. This formula in turn frames single meanders and double meanders twice each. Still other formulas can be discerned in this fabric, which increases in complexity as it nears the handle zone of the vase—the most important zone—and then contracts again. It is clear that the surface is ordered through the elaborate rhythmic repetition of distinct parts—that it is, in short, tectonically and formulaically composed.

This is one of several ways in which the Dipylon style and the Homeric style appear to be parallel. In both, the formula—not the single word, not the single brush stroke—is the basic compositional unit. The poet, using verbal blocks that can be as short as two words or as long as thirty-five lines (compare, for instance bk. 9, ll. 122–57 and bk. 9, ll. 264–99) but are all pressed into the rhythmic frame of the hexameter, is as much a builder of narrative surfaces as the vase painter is of decorative surfaces (and *tektōn epeōn,* "builder of words," is just how the Greeks could conceive of their poets). The formula, oral or geometric, is both the tool and the stuff of the construction, and it lends to both monumental epic and monumental vase the qualities of stability and unity. For Homer's audience the formula was an aid to recognition: one use of a formula predicts or recalls other uses of the formula. Any line of oral poetry must have *seemed* familiar and equal, even if it was mostly new (similarly, whole episodes or tales can seem familiar because they make use of certain narrative themes or patterns). Formulaic language is highly resonant language, alluding constantly to itself. And thus the narrative moment, which is in fact fleeting, takes on the sturdy character of the regular, the constant, and the predictable. In a sense, the very language of Homer is its own meaning: it is the embodiment and validation of order itself. And just as oral formulae and thematic patterns guided the ear through the intricate texture of epic song, so the visual formulae employed by the Dipylon Master guide the spectator's eye over the huge surface of the amphora: one use of a motif echoes another and the additive surface coheres. In the geometric medium lies a message of order.

Figures that are treated formulaically become archetypes, schemata. The deer that graze and the goats that kneel on the neck of Athens 804—they take part in the first two continuous animal friezes in Archaic art (thousands more will follow)—are so treated. The animals in each frieze are identical. They are there, in fact, less as animals than as pattern, and they do not function differently from the bands of abstract ornament above and below (the goats, for instance, turn their heads back upon themselves, seeming to mimic the design of the meander). There is some variation among the thirty-nine human figures who inhabit the handle zone of the amphora—eight in a panel on the back, six under each handle, nineteen in the commanding *prothesis* on the front—but there is not much. In the *prothesis*, the limp-wristed corpse—she is at the exact center of the entire vase—and the two reclining women beneath her apparently wear gowns. A figure on a stool gestures with her hand. A child is a miniature adult. Two figures at the far left wear swords (and so they are men) and raise one arm in mourning. But the distinctions are minute: the Dipylon Master's mostly nude figures, male and female, on all seven of the vases attributed to him (nearly fifty more are assigned to other members of his shop) are essentially the same figure. The continuous, fleshy contours and irregular, relatively naturalistic proportions of earlier silhouettes have been rejected. Instead, the figure has been broken down into separate abstract shapes and, like the amphora itself, has been subjected to the ordering force of a proportional canon. The head is a tiny circle with a large lump for a chin, but the height of the head and the shaftlike neck together is one-half the height of the torso. The torso (shown frontally) is a tall and precise triangle precisely extrapolated by the muscleless sticks that serve for arms. The body is nearly cut in thirds at the waist (or at least at the spot where the waist should be) and at the knees: the distances between waist and knee and between knee and foot are virtually identical, and so are the curves of thigh and calf. All in all, the Dipylon silhouette, whose joints do not so much connect as exaggerate divisions, is the sum of distinct but mathematically related parts. It is structured according to a 1/2:1:1:1 ratio: the head (and neck) is one-seventh the height of the entire figure—a precociously classical scheme. The unity of the figure is at any rate of a special sort: it is structural or tectonic, not organic, and the segment matters as much as the synthesis.

In this respect the Dipylon and Homeric conceptions of the human form may be cognate. Long ago, Bruno Snell argued that Homer has no one word for the body (or the mind or the soul) of a living person—one has a body (*sōma*) only when one is dead—and that Homer could thus have had no notion of the body (or the mind or the soul) as a whole. Physically the Homeric human being is, Snell argued, as much a composite of head, chest, and limbs as a Dipylon silhouette: thus Akhilleus can say "my arms" have fought when he means "I" (bk. 1, l. 166). Emotionally and intellectually, too, Snell's Homeric human is an aggregate of distinct "organs": thus Odysseus can talk to his own *thymos,* that part of his soul concerned with temper and emotion, as if it were outside of him (bk. 11, ll. 403–10). Snell's thesis is not perfect: he does not say why a corpse can have (or be) a "body" but a living person cannot, and there are apparently a few exceptions to the rule in any case. It is also true that not all Late Geometric artists present so schematic and tectonic a view of the human form as the Dipylon Master: though their medium undoubtedly had something to do with it, the makers of bronze statuettes could create particularly rubbery and inarticulate figures that have little to do with the Dipylon aesthetic. Nonetheless, the Dipylon Master and Homer—the greatest artist and the greatest poet of their age—both generally conceived of the human form in pieces and as pieces.

The Dipylon figure—a formulaic attachment of part to part—conveys information. It tells what makes up a human being. It tells what all human beings are like by eliminating (or ignoring) the peculiarities of individual members of the species. The Dipylon figure, in other words, expresses what is constant about the human form, not what is fleeting; what is essential, not what is idiosyncratic. Human beings are as changeable and as transient as the leaves Homer compares them to (bk. 6, ll. 146–49, bk. 21, ll. 464–66), but the *idea* of a human being—a creature with a blob for a head, a triangle for a chest, two legs, and two arms—is not. And it is a similar yearning for the essential, a similar impulse for the archetypal, that is expressed by the Homeric epithet—a descriptive word (or two) that helps fill out the hexameter line like an ornament but that also establishes what is constant and unchanging about a character or a thing. Dawn is early-born and rosy-fingered, ships are swift or black, women are white-armed, Hera is queenly and thus golden-throned even when she is lying down (bk. 1, l. 611), Akhilleus is swift-footed even when he is sitting still (bk. 16, l. 5). Homer's characters, of course, differ from one another; the Dipylon Master's silhouettes differ hardly at all. Still, epithets regularly appended to names and objects help place them beyond the realm of change. The epithet-noun formula, like the formulae the Dipylon Master drew, seeks to exclude what is atypical and affirm what is permanent. Homeric diction and the Dipylon figured style share an abhorrence of the accidental and mutable.

A particular view of reality is shared besides. For the performing Homer, reality was whatever he was singing at the time, and his conception of reality—that is, his representation of it—was thus necessarily bound to his narrative medium and organizational methods. Two of his most important devices are symmetry and antithesis, devices that order because they arrange, enclose, and frame. The impulse for symmetry can be seen in a single line—for instance, the line that summarizes what it is to be a Homeric hero: *mythōn te rētēr' emenai prēktēra te ergōn* (bk. 9, l. 443). The verse means "to be a speaker of words and a doer of deeds," but in the Greek "of words" (*mythōn*) at the beginning of the line is balanced by "of deeds" (*ergōn*) at the end, "speaker" (*rētēr'*) is balanced by "doer" (*prēktēra*), and "to be" (*emenai*) occupies dead center. This kind of symmetry, in which the order of words in parallel clauses is inverted, is known as *chiasmos,* and the same antithetical (and mnemonic) principle governs whole passages as well. When in the underworld Odysseus asks the shade of his mother a series of questions about her death and the situation back home on Ithaka, she answers them in reverse order, last question first (*Odyssey,* bk. 11, ll. 171–203). The *Iliad* itself, in fact, is framed by a vast *chiasmos.* Book 1 begins with a nine-day-long plague and mass burials and continues with Akhilleus's quarrel with Agamemnon, Thetis's visits to Akhilleus and Zeus, and finally an argument among the gods. Book 24 begins with an argument among the gods and continues with Thetis's visits to Zeus and Akhilleus, the reconciliation between Akhilleus and Priam (antithetical to the quarrel with Agamemnon in book 1), and finally a nine-day-long truce for Hektor's burial. The principles of antithesis and symmetry have seemed so pervasive and authoritative to some scholars that they consider the *Iliad* the poetic equivalent of a Late Geometric amphora, designed with as much concern for abstract form as, say, the surface of Athens 804. To say that every episode, every narrative part, is precisely balanced by another is to go too far: the "geometry" of the *Iliad* is not so pure. But there *are* plenty of symmetries and patterns to be found. This symmetry, together with the strong and gratifying sense that the epic finishes what it starts (its sense of closure), is as much a manifestation of order as the formula itself, and it is as much a manifestation of order as the tightly organized works of the finest Late Geometric vase painter—or the Shield of Akhilleus. Homer may never have seen a vase of the quality of a Dipylon amphora. The Dipylon Master may never have heard Homer's *Iliad.* But there is nothing unreasonable about looking at, say, the Dipylon Master's *prothesis* (where mourners balance each other around the central bier and neatly fill their rectangular panel, holding their arms exactly parallel to the upper border) and detecting analogous impulses for symmetry and closure. Whether expressed in words or in images, these impulses are symptoms of a larger Late Geometric mentality that revered stability and finality—the values of order—and that perfected poetic and artistic structures to control the world and put its parts in their places.

The parts are generally set side by side. Perhaps even more fundamental to the Homeric and Late Geometric representations of reality than symmetry is parataxis, a style in which sentences, ideas, episodes, or figures are placed one after the other like beads on a string. In paratactic narrative, every idea, every scene seems independent and equal to every other— equally important, equally emphasized—and thus all seem to exist on one uniform level or plane. The planar quality of the Homeric style is particularly evident in so-called digressions, long (but hardly irrelevant) passages that interrupt the narrative and occupy the listener so completely that the matter at hand is momentarily lost. Digressions typically occur at times of tension or high drama—for instance, in the heat of battle, where a charge of chariots can be stopped by a long genealogy (bk. 6, ll. 145–211), or where a simile used to describe a bloody wound becomes a thing apart, and the wound is for a few lines forgotten (bk. 4, ll. 141–45). The most famous digression is the tale of Odysseus's scar in book 19 of the *Odyssey*. Penelope has told the old nurse Eurykleia to wash Odysseus's feet (he is in disguise). She uncovers his leg, touches his scar, and at once recognizes her master. But her reaction is delayed for more than seventy lines while Homer tells how Odysseus got his name and how he got the scar in a boar hunt on Mount Parnassos (ll. 393–466). Only after the digression does Eurykleia finally drop her master's leg into the washbasin and exclaim, "You are Odysseus!" As Erich Auerbach has argued, this and other digressions are not there to relieve tension but to elucidate. They are characteristic of the Homeric impulse to leave nothing obscure: if Odysseus has a scar, the reason for it must be explained. Past events and experiences, even motivation and thought processes, are clearly expressed or externalized (cf. bk. 11, ll. 403–10). All phenomena are thrust forward to the narrative surface—to the foreground—where they receive even, objective illumination. No hidden depths exist; nothing is omitted, vague, or darkly imaginable. There is, we may say, no perspective in the style of narrative Auerbach has identified—nothing that is subordinate, nothing that does not exist on the front plane of the epic. And this paratactic presentation of everything, everyone, and every thought was undoubtedly conditioned by the nature of oral performance, where there was only the sound of the words, where each hexameter, once heard, was gone and replaced by another of equal grammatical and semantic value. Homeric reality was in effect the narrative moment—a flat, continuous present.

Parataxis and the plane control Late Geometric artistic representations of reality as well. Like each excessively jointed Dipylon silhouette—Paratactic Man if there ever was one—the entire *prothesis* on Athens 804 is a flat alignment of parts. It consists, first, of distinct groups of figures—those to the left of the bier, those to the right, and those below—but each figure is in fact independent, set off from its neighbor by vertical stacks of zigzags. This so-called filling ornament—something that was substantially missing in earlier scenes—blends the picture with the abstract fabric beyond its borders: it is stitching, and it reduces the harshness of what would otherwise have been an airy, light patch suspended in a dense geometric tapestry. But this is not all that the filler does: it also assigns each mourner a separate and equal place on the surface of the vase. Each figure is clearly framed: overlapping of figures is strictly prohibited because it would obscure the contours of the silhouettes and cause visual confusion. Even the dead noblewoman is completely visible: the checkered shroud that in reality covered her is apparently held above, and it is cut back so as not to muddle her outline—it is almost as if we are allowed to see through the cloth rather than peek beneath it. The Late Geometric representation of reality aims for clarity, comprehension, and objectivity above all. The corpse is exposed because it is known to be there: to cover it up would be, somehow, dishonest or deceptive. The other figures are objectively equal: therefore they must be equally intelligible and therefore they must exist on the same plane, in the foreground. The mourners who in the painting antithetically flank the funeral couch in reality probably circled it in ritual lamentation. The dance, which would have obscured the bier as it passed in front and been obscured by the bier as it passed behind, has been cut in two and its halves have been stretched across the surface to form, paratactically, two human colonnades. Similarly, mourners did not really sit beneath the bier but in front of it, yet they are made to inhabit the same plane as the corpse and the standing mourners. Even when the Dipylon Master populated a much larger pictorial field with a much larger cast, we see the same flattening of space, the same projection of parts onto the regular, front plane. The row of mourners who sit, impossibly, atop the shroud of the deceased on a fragmentary krater in the Louvre actually sat behind the bier, and the bier was really behind the tall mourners who stand comfortably under it. The four smaller mourners who seem to stand precariously on top of each other on either side of the bier are not really circus acrobats: the ones on top are to be thought of as standing behind those on the bottom. The rule that what is above was in fact behind is loose, but it is one of the very few in Late Geometric art, and it was formulated because no distance or depth, no perspective, could be allowed to intrude into—and thus weaken—the Late Geometric conception of reality. Nothing (or almost nothing) can be hidden or implicit. Geometric space, like the Homeric representation of reality, essentially consists of a uniformly illuminated foreground. The picture plane does not merely *contain* a representation of reality, it is the *equivalent* of reality.

A painted vase, no matter how fine, large, or intricately decorated, is not an epic poem. A sparse *prothesis* cannot compare with the rich, tragic complexity of the *Iliad*. A schematic silhouette cannot possess the mighty character and depth of an Akhilleus. The Dipylon Master did not attempt to compete with Homer or reproduce the *Iliad* in clay and glaze, and parallels between Homer and other Late Geometric artists do not hold so well. Yet it is stranger to treat Homeric epic and the Dipylon style in total isolation than it is to see in them a rare spectacle of unity. In their delight in sheer size, in their tightly controlled use of formulae to construct monumental, highly patterned, and well-proportioned edifices, in their use of archetypes to counter the multiplicity and mutability of things, in their conception of the body as a summary of parts, in their dependence on symmetry and antithesis as means of arranging the world, in their powerful sense of closure, and in their paratactic projection (or refraction) of reality upon the flat plane of the foreground, the Dipylon style and Homeric narrative are related manifestations of the subliminal impulses, the ordered sensibility, of the culture of mid-eighth-century Greece—a culture that after the final dissipation of the Dark Age sought through both its art and its poetry to reinforce its beliefs and confirm its rigorous vision of the world.

Chronology

ca. 4000 B.C.	Dawn of Bronze Age in Crete.
ca. 3000 B.C.	Beginning of northern invasions of Greece.
ca. 2000 B.C.	Unification of Minoan power in Crete.
ca. 2000–1700 B.C.	Achaean invasion.
ca. 1600 B.C.	Destruction of Phaestos and Cnossos in Crete. Palaces rebuilt. Greek linear script replaces hieroglyphs.
ca. 1600–1400 B.C.	Strong Cretan influence in Greece. The shaft-grave dynasty in Mycenae.
ca. 1400 B.C.	Second destruction of Cretan palaces. Rapid wane of Minoan power.
ca. 1400–1200 B.C.	Great age of Mycenae. Development of Mycenaean trade in Egypt and Eastern Mediterranean. Trade with the West.
1287 B.C.	Battle of Cadesh between Egypt and Hittites; decline of both powers.
ca. 1250–1240 B.C.	Trojan War.
ca. 1180 B.C.	Troy destroyed by Mycenaeans.
ca. 1150 B.C.	Destruction of Mycenaean centers in Greece.
ca. 1100 B.C.	Successive waves of Dorian invaders penetrate Greece. "Dark Age" begins. Use of iron introduced.
ca. 800–500 B.C.	Development of the city-state from monarchy. Ionian School of lyric poetry.
776 B.C.	First Olympic Festival.
ca. 750–650 B.C.	Composition of *Iliad* and *Odyssey*.

Contributors

HAROLD BLOOM, Sterling Professor of the Humanities at Yale University, is the author of *The Anxiety of Influence, Poetry and Repression,* and many other volumes of literary criticism. A MacArthur Prize Fellow, he is general editor of the series of literary criticism published by Chelsea House.

E. R. DODDS was Regius Professor of Greek at Oxford University and the author of *The Greeks and the Irrational* and *The Ancient Concept of Progress.*

CEDRIC H. WHITMAN was Eliot Professor of Greek at Harvard University at his death in 1978.

BRUNO SNELL is one of the major European scholars of classical literature. His book *The Discovery of the Mind* is a comprehensive study of the tradition that goes from Homer through Virgil.

ERIC A. HAVELOCK is Sterling Professor of Classics Emeritus at Yale University.

JAMES M. REDFIELD teaches at the University of Chicago, with appointments to the Committee on Social Thought, the Department of Classical Languages and Literatures, and the College.

GREGORY NAGY is Professor of Greek and Latin at Harvard University.

JEFFREY M. HURWIT is Professor of Art History at the University of Oregon.

Bibliography

Adkins, A. W. H. "Homeric Values and Homeric Society." *Journal of Hellenic Studies* 91 (1971): 1–14.

Amory, Anne. "Blameless Aegisthus." *Mnemosyne,* supp. vol. 26 (1973).

Armstrong, J. "The Arming Motif in the *Iliad.*" *American Journal of Philology* 79 (1958): 337–54.

Bespaloff, Rachel. *On the* Iliad. New York: Harper Torchbooks, 1947.

Bowra, C. M. *Traditions and Design in the* Iliad. Oxford: Oxford University Press, 1930.

Burkert, Walter. "Apellai und Apollon." *Rheinisches Museum* 118 (1975): 1–21.

Carpenter, Rhys. *Folktale, Fiction and Saga in the Homeric Epics.* Berkeley: University of California Press, 1946.

Dodds, E. R. *The Greeks and the Irrational.* Berkeley: University of California Press, 1951.

Eichholz, D. E. "The Propitiation of Achilles." *American Journal of Philology* 74 (1953): 137–48.

Fenik, Bernard, ed. *Homer: Tradition and Invention.* Cincinnati Classical Studies, vol. 2. Leiden, Netherlands: Brill, 1978.

Frankel, Hermann. *Early Greek Poetry and Philosophy: A History of Greek Epic, Lyric and Prose to the Middle of the Fifth Century.* Translated by Moses Hadas and James Willis. New York: Harcourt Brace Jovanovich, 1973.

Greene, Thomas M. *The Descent from Heaven: A Study in Epic Continuity.* New Haven: Yale University Press, 1963.

Griffin, Jasper. *Homer on Life and Death.* Oxford: Clarendon, 1980.

Kirk, G. S. *Homer and the Oral Tradition.* Cambridge: Cambridge University Press, 1978.

———. *The Iliad: A Commentary.* Vol. 1, Books 1–4. Cambridge: Cambridge University Press, 1985.

———. *The Songs of Homer.* Cambridge: Cambridge University Press, 1962.

Lesky, Albin. *Gottliche und Menschliche Motivation in Homerischen Epos.* Sitzungsberichte der Heidelberger Akademie der Wissenschaften Philosophisch-Historische Klasse, Vol. 4. Heidelberg: C. Winter, 1961.

Moulton, Carroll. "Homeric Metaphor." *Classical Philology* 74 (1979): 279–93.

Mueller, Martin. *The Iliad.* London: Allen & Unwin, 1984.

Otto, Walter F. *The Homeric Gods.* Translated by Moses Hadas. New York: Pantheon, 1954.

Parry, Adam. "Have We Homer's *Iliad?*" *Yale Classical Studies* 20 (1966): 175–216.

Parry, Milman. *The Making of Homeric Verse.* Oxford: Oxford University Press, 1971.

Scodel, Ruth. "The Autobiography of Phoenix: *Iliad* 9:444–95." *American Journal of Philology* 103 (1982): 128–36.

Segal, Charles. "The Theme of the Mutilation of the Corpse in the *Iliad.*" *Mnemosyne,* supp. vol. 17 (1971).

Snell, Bruno. *The Discovery of the Mind: The Greek Origins of European Thought.* Translated by T. G. Rosenmeyer. New York: Harper & Row, 1960.

Snodgrass, A. M. "An Historical Homeric Society." *Journal of Hellenic Studies* 94 (1974): 114–25.

Vivante, Paolo. *Homer.* New Haven: Yale University Press, 1985.

Wade-Gery, H. T. *The Poet of the* Iliad. Cambridge: Cambridge University Press, 1952.

Acknowledgments

"Agamemnon's Apology" by E. R. Dodds from *The Greeks and the Irrational* by E. R. Dodds, © 1951 by the Regents of the University of California. Reprinted by permission of the University of California Press.

"Homeric Character and the Tradition" by Cedric H. Whitman from *Homer and the Heroic Tradition* by Cedric H. Whitman, © 1958 by the President and Fellows of Harvard College. Reprinted by permission of Harvard University Press.

"Homer's View of Man" by Bruno Snell from *The Discovery of the Mind: The Greek Origins of European Thought* by Bruno Snell, translated by T. G. Rosenmeyer, © 1953 by Basil Blackwell Publishers. Reprinted by permission.

"The Homeric State of Mind" by Eric A. Havelock from *Preface to Plato* by Eric A. Havelock, © 1963 by the President and Fellows of Harvard College. Reprinted by permission of Harvard University Press.

"Nature and Culture in the *Iliad*: Purification" (originally entitled "Purification") by James M. Redfield from *Nature and Culture in the* Iliad: *The Tragedy of Hector* by James M. Redfield, © 1975 by the University of Chicago. Reprinted by permission of the University of Chicago Press.

"Some Elements of the Homeric Fantasy" by Eric A. Havelock from *The Greek Concept of Justice: From Its Shadow in Homer to Its Substance in Plato* by Eric A. Havelock, © 1978 by Eric A. Havelock. Reprinted by permission of the author and Harvard University Press.

"Poetic Visions of Immortality for the Hero" by Gregory Nagy from *The Best of the Achaeans: Concepts of the Hero in Archaic Greek Poetry* by Gregory Nagy, © 1979 by the Johns Hopkins University Press, Baltimore/London. Reprinted by permission.

"Formula and Foreground: Homer and the Dipylon Style" (originally entitled "The Idea of Order, 760–700: Formula and Foreground: Homer and the Dipylon Style") by Jeffrey M. Hurwit from *The Art and Culture of Early Greece, 1100–480 B.C.* by Jeffrey M. Hurwit, © 1985 by Cornell University. Reprinted by permission of Cornell University Press.

Index

Achilles, 35, 43, 80–81, 93, 94, 98, 139, 140, 141, 143; and Agamemnon, 27, 46–47, 99–100, 104, 141; and *aidôs*, 41; and Ajax of Salamis, 41; *aristeia* of, 30, 36; on *atē*, 12; character of, 3, 4–6, 21, 27–28, 30, 44, 47–48, 82, 84, 90; compared to David (Old Testament), 4–5; compared to Demophon, 117–18, 120–21; compared to Odysseus, 45–48; death of, 39; evolution of character of, 46–47; as focal character in *Iliad*, 43, 79; funeral of, 112–13, 134; and the gods, 80–82, 90; and Hector, 79–81, 84, 91–92; as hero, 90–92, 106–7, 117–18; as heroic ideal, 43; and immortality, 112–13, 134; and killing of Lycaon, 30; as member of community of gods, 82; mortality of, 116–17; Muses and death of, 112–13, 117; nature of, 7–8, 89, 91–92; oath of, 115, 120; origin of name of, 113; and Patroclus, 32, 76, 78, 79–80, 84; Pindar and theme of, 112–13; Priam's submission to, 83–84; purification of, 87; and ransoming of Hector, 82–87, 90; and relationship to Priam, 28, 83–87, 88, 98, 141; and role in *Odyssey*, 47–48; sceptre of, 31; self-realization by, 86–87; and Thetis, 121; as tragic character, 36; under influence of monition, 20; world view of, 43, 48; and wrestling match between Odysseus and Ajax of Salamis, 39; and Zeus, 42

Action: archetypes in *Iliad*, 26; as related to form, 88–89

Aeneas, 35, 37, 38, 43

Aeschylus, and relationship between Erinys and *moira*, 16

Agamemnon, 35, 87, 91, 98, 104; and Achilles, 27, 46–47, 99–100, 104, 141; *aristeia* of, 29–30; as *basileus*, 99–100; character of, 21, 27–29, 30–33, 43; and Diomedes, 29; exaggerated personal status of, 97; in the Great Battle, 29–30; insecurity of, 32; as materialist, 27–28; and Menelaus, 32; and relationship to Odysseus, 29, 44–45, 94; sceptre of, 30–31; *skēptron* of, and nature imagery, 114–15, 120; and Teucer, 32; as tragic character, 32–33; under influence of *atē*, 12, 23; wounding of, 29–30, 41

Agora, as related to *megaron*, 105

Aidôs, 81; Achilles and, 41; Ajax of Salamis and, 40–41, 42, 43; Antilichus and, 40; Hector and, 40; Menelaus and, 40; nature of, 40

Ajax of Locris, 34, 43

Ajax of Salamis, 30, 35, 72, 93; and Achilles, 41; and *aidôs*, 40–41, 42, 43; character of, 21, 39–41, 42, 44; compared to Diomedes, 35; and death of Achilles, 39; and death of Patroclus, 39; in the Great Battle, 40; as heroic ideal, 35, 40–41; Homer's development of character of, 42; lack of *aristeia* of, 38; prayer for death of, 32; traditional stories about, 38–39; as tragic character, 42; and wres-